## WONDERFUL WORLD OF KNOWLEDGE

Exploration and Discovery

# Disney's Wonderful World of Knowledge

THE DANBURY PRESS

THE DANBURY PRESS

*a division of Grolier Enterprises, Inc.*

Robert B. Clarke        *Publisher*

ARNOLDO MONDADORI EDITORE

Mario Gentilini              *Editor-in-Chief*
Elisa Penna                  *Supervising Editor*
Giovan Battista Carpi        *Illustrators*
Claudio Mazzoli
Guido Martina                *Author*

"Disney's wonderful world of knowledge"
is an updated and enlarged English version of
an encyclopedia heretofore printed in the Italian language by
arnoldo mondadori editore, milan
and entitled (in English Translation) "Disney encyclopedia"

© 1971, 1973 Walt Disney Productions        **Printed in the United States of America**

All rights reserved.                                                8998

Library of Congress Catalog Card No. 73-12816

# CONTENTS

THE WORLD OPENS UP   9
    The Land of Punt   9
    Cosmetics for the Queen   11
    Men From the Land of Purple   12
    The Carthaginians   15
    In the Name of Honesty   15
    Venture to the North   16

WORLDS AT THEIR FEET   19
    The Birth of a Leader   20
    A Kingdom for a Prince   22
    The Great Adventure   24
    Trial by Fire   25
    A Legend for the Ages   26
    An Emperor and His Empire   28
    The Past is Unlocked   30
    Digging for History   32
    The City of a Thousand Columns   36

EXPLORERS AND NAVIGATORS   39
    The Bold Vikings   41
    The Vikings Discover America   44
    Marco Polo   46
    Admiral of the Ocean Sea   54
    The Story of an Error   54
    August 3, 1492   60
    The Road to the Indies   66

    The First Voyage Around the World   70
    The Man Who Searched for the Stars   74
    In Darkest Africa   77
    A Time of Hardship   78
    "Dr. Livingstone, I Presume?"   78
    Exploring the Arctic   82
    Fridtjof Nansen   83
    A Dangerous Journey   84
    Riding the Wind   86
    Peary Conquers the Pole   88
    Over and Under The Pole   90
    Exploring the Antarctic   94
    White Death   98

SCALING THE ROOF OF THE WORLD   105
    From the Heavens to the Depths of the Sea   108
    The Adventures of the *Kon-Tiki* and the *Ra*   110

A PATHWAY THROUGH THE SKIES   115
    Man Flies   117
    The Lone Eagle   118
    The Moon is Near   121
    The Moon is Ours!   123
    Index   124

# THE WORLD OPENS UP

Hello, boys and girls, this is your old friend, Mickey Mouse. I've come to take you on a glorious and thrilling adventure. Want to go? I hear all your excited voices shouting yes, yes, yes! Good. Now let's close our eyes tightly, only for a moment. Okay? Imagine that we are going backward in time. Back, back through the centuries, through thousands upon thousands of years, till we are at the age of man's first appearance on earth. We are in a mysterious and unfriendly world. A world filled with wild beasts and many enemies.

Just a few seconds longer in this strange and frightening world. Now we shall leave it. Let's open our eyes and we are back in our modern world. Man is no longer filled with fears because he knows his world and how to live in it. Now I, Mickey Mouse, invite you to walk the road of time with me. I'm going to tell you how, when, and why man began to look beyond the horizon and to enlarge the limits of his tiny world.

There is neither time nor space enough for all the things I want to tell you. So I shall have to skip from the caveman period to the time when man started to venture into the great unknown: the sea.

## THE LAND OF PUNT

Boys and girls, I'm going to start with the Egyptians who lived thousands of years ago. The ancient Egyptians were mainly an agricultural people. They were not great sailors. Their frail boats, tiny crafts built of small planks, could not face the open sea. So the Egyptians wisely chose dry land for their trading activities. They formed caravans that followed the course of the Nile River until it reached the Sudan, a country just south of Egypt. There the traders exchanged Egyptian goods for ebony, ivory, perfumed oils, and ostrich plumes. The men who made up these caravans were really the first explorers of the interior of Africa.

And yet, strange as it may seem, it was the people of this land who carried out the first and quite daring seagoing explorations along the African coasts. An expedition was sent into unknown lands about 2550 B.C. The purpose of the expedition was to "guide ships to the Land of Punt." (Punt is present-day Somalia, a country in eastern Africa.) An Egyptian nobleman named Henu was the leader of the venture. His caravans crossed the vast desert wasteland and then reached

*Left: A group of Egyptian wooden soldiers from the 22nd century* B.C.
*Above: A bas-relief showing the Queen of Punt, followed by bearers of precious goods. It was found in the Temple of Hatshepsut, the Egyptian queen who sent an expedition to bring back the rare products of Punt.*

Sheba on the Red Sea. There Henu set to work to build the ships that he was to lead to the Land of Punt and other lands. When the fleet was built, Henu and his men set sail and pushed their way into the distant seas. They visited far-off lands and eventually came home loaded with foreign goods. Henu is now thought of as one of the first commanders of an important seaborn commercial expedition.

## COSMETICS FOR THE QUEEN

A thousand years after Henu's sea adventure, the Egyptian Queen Hatshepsut sent a fleet of five ships to Punt. Their mission was to bring back to Egypt "all the perfumed woods of the land, trees and resins of myrrh, ebony, solid ivory, green gold, cinnamon wood, two qualities of

incense, eye cosmetics and also monkeys, dogs, panther skins, as well as natives with their children."

That's really some list, isn't it, boys and girls? And what do you think of the queen especially ordering cosmetics for herself? Please don't tell Minnie Mouse about this. She's an awfully sweet girl and all that, but in my humble opinion I think she is too fond of perfume and powder and all that stuff. There's a good chance that I'm going to be sent to Africa to track down some jewel thieves. If Minnie hears about Queen Hatshepsut and her eye cosmetics and the perfumes... well, she'd surely insist that I bring back a plane full of perfumes for her.

Queen Hatshepsut is also remembered for having sent out another expedition. This expedition sailed down the Nile for many miles. It brought back an obelisk, a tall pillar of stone shaped at top like a pyramid. The obelisk stood in front of the temple of Amon near Thebes. Unfortunately the obelisk was destroyed.

## MEN FROM THE LAND OF PURPLE

During the reign of Queen Hatshepsut

*Shipbuilding in the Phoenician port city of Tyre about 1,000 B.C. The workers are using planks of Lebanese cedar. Tyre, at the eastern end of the Mediterranean, withstood invasion for centuries.*

another people was sending their ships out of home ports. These were the brave and hardy Phoenicians. They have gone down in history as a nation of great sailors and navigators. Many historians rank the Phoenicians as the greatest seamen of the ancient world.

Their name, which was given to them by the Greeks, means "red-skinned men" or perhaps "men from the land of purple." The Phoenicians were great exporters of a purple dye that they extracted from a snail. Since about 4000 B.C. the Phoenicians lived along the Syrian coasts between the sea and the Lebanese mountains. Great forests of cedar furnished them with wood for their ships. The purple dye was used for coloring their sails. At a very early stage in their nation's history, the Phoenicians began to sail out into the Mediterranean Sea. After a while these brave sailors became masters of this historic sea—a body of water that has played an extremely important role in man's history and continues to do so today.

Whenever the Phoenicians found a land that was rich in trading goods or in a commercial location, they left a few people there. Gradually they set up the foundations for a Phoenician colony. In this way they knew they were establishing bases where they could be safe from their enemies.

While on long voyages they could plan to stop at these bases and rest for a few days, pick up needed supplies, and then go on again. Carthage, Cadiz, Utica, and Palermo were all Phoenician colonies. They were founded at different periods. In due time every one of these colonies grew and prospered.

Some historians believe that the first large expedition carried out by the Phoenicians was organized by an Egyptian Pharaoh who reigned during the 6th century B.C. He is said to have formulated a plan to connect the Nile with the Red Sea. He called together some of the best Phoenician sailors and persuaded them to go on this adventure. They were to sail around the continent of Africa. The Greek historian Herodotus, who is called the father of history, wrote an account of this expedition.

Sailing from the Red Sea these sailors went onto the Aystral Sea (that is, the Indian Ocean), landing every autumn to plant crops and then await the harvests. After 3 years of travel they returned to Egypt, where they told extraordinary tales of their voyage. No one believed a word of what they said. For example, they claimed that at one point of their voyage the sun suddenly rose on their right. This tale was called a lie. But it makes us believe that these sailors actually went around the Cape of Good Hope. When they rounded the Cape they were sailing northward and so had the east on their right. When sailing southward they naturally had the rising sun on their left.

The Phoenicians did not like to sail in the open sea. They preferred to travel

along the coasts, guiding themselves during the long nights by the North Star.

## THE CARTHAGINIANS

According to ancient reports, Carthage was established along the coast of North Africa sometime in the 8th century B.C. This was during the reign of the legendary Queen Dido. Carthage's location on the Mediterranean Sea helped to make it a powerful commercial center. For various trading reasons the Carthaginians were greatly interested in going completely around the African continent. They set up an expedition that was put in the charge of an excellent navigator named Sataspes. At that time Sataspes was a criminal who had been condemned to death. However, he was promised a pardon if his voyage was successful.

Sataspes left Carthage, but after sailing for several months along the coast, he was finally forced to turn back because of extremely bad weather. Discouraged, he returned to Carthage and told of having visited a land inhabited by black men who raised cattle and who dressed themselves in palm leaves. It is quite possible that he had reached the coast of Guinea. But since his mission was a failure, he was put to death.

Another Carthaginian, Hanno, had better luck. Near the end of the 5th century B.C. he sailed with a fleet of 60 ships to set up colonies along the coast of West

*The ruins of Carthage, near present-day Tunis. Phoenicians from Tyre founded Carthage on the coast of North Africa about 814 B.C. It grew to be the greatest of all Phoenician colonies, even more splendid and powerful than Tyre. Rome and Carthage became enemies, and in the Third Punic War, Rome defeated Carthage. The Romans leveled the city, ploughed up the ground, and sold the survivors as slaves. But Rome later rebuilt Carthage, and it is the remains of Roman buildings we see today.*

Africa. He left his homeland with about 30,000 colonists, both men and women. They were settled in various spots along the coast. This was one of the most important colonizing efforts of ancient times. Hanno tells that during his voyage he came upon "savage men whose bodies were completely covered with hair and who spoke an incomprehensible language. We could not capture the men because they defended themselves by throwing stones at us. We did succeed in capturing three women, but they would not follow us and scratched and bit us...." We know that these savage men and women were none other than apes or gorillas!

## IN THE NAME OF HONESTY

The Carthaginians gained a reputation for being fair and honest in their dealings with other peoples. The historian Herodotus writes about the Carthaginians and their trading practices. He tells that

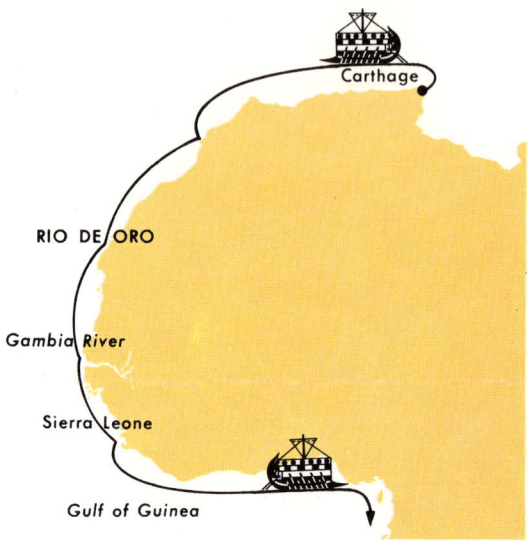

*Above: Route followed by the Carthaginian navigator Hanno when he sailed down the west coast of Africa in the 6th or 5th century B.C. His expedition, made up of 60 ships and 30,000 persons, settled in several coastal areas.*

*Below: The voyage of the Greek explorer Pytheas, who sailed out of the Mediterranean Sea north to England and probably to Norway (Thule). He described the frozen ocean, but no one believed him.*

in the course of their voyages along the western African coast, the Carthaginians upon reaching land unloaded their merchandise and arranged it in an orderly fashion on the beach. They then went back to their ships. From their ships they sent up a huge smoke signal that could be seen from a great distance. Upon seeing this smoke the people of the vicinity hurried to the beach. They looked at the merchandise and left gold in payment. They then withdrew to a certain distance. The Carthaginians returned to the shore and if, in their opinion, the gold was enough to cover the value of the merchandise, they took the gold aboard and continued on their journey. If, however, they thought the gold was not enough, they went back to their ships and waited. The people returned and added more gold until the sellers were satisfied. The Carthaginians never touched the gold until it equaled what they considered the value of their goods. The people of the land never moved the merchandise from its spot until the traders took the gold and departed. Each side acted with complete faith and honesty toward the other.

## VENTURE TO THE NORTH

Until now your old friend, Mickey Mouse, has been telling you about men who traveled for commercial reasons. But now I'm going to introduce you to a new kind of adventurer—one who voyaged in order to discover new lands and so add to the knowledge of his fellow man. Let's meet the noble explorer Pytheas.

Pytheas was a Greek scholar who was born in a Greek colony called Massalia. Massalia is now the French port city of Marseilles. Pytheas must have been a rich man, certainly not as rich as Uncle

A Hittite bas-relief of the 8th century B.C. showing a Phoenician ship that uses sail and oars. The pilot stands aft and manages the large oar that serves as a rudder. The captain stands in the prow.

Scrooge, but sufficiently well off to enable him to outfit a ship at his own expense. Sometime about 325 B.C. Pytheas sailed from Massalia and finally landed somewhere in the British Isles. He later wrote about this trip and described the climate and inhabitants of the land. He sailed farther north into icy seas and discovered the island of Thule. Some modern geographers believe that Pytheas really discovered Norway. Others think that he sighted Denmark and Sweden. Pytheas added to man's knowledge. He learned to establish distance and direction accurately by observing the height of the sun at noon. He wrote two important books, *On the Ocean* and *Circumnavigation*. The books were eventually lost, but geographers of that time made good use of the material that was in them. Greek map makers also relied heavily on Pytheas.

# WORLDS AT THEIR FEET

I'm sure you know the names of some of the great generals of history. You probably also have read stories about their exciting adventures. You should not forget, however, that not all battles were fought for good reasons or with good results for the world. Some conquests were born only of ambition.

But enough of this! Pluto's tail tells me that he is tired of listening to a sermon. A man who leads armies to victory is without doubt a great general. There have been a few men, and only a few, who in addition to being great generals were truly great men. Two leaders especially, Alexander the Great and Julius Caesar, had burning ambitions to rule the world. But they also dreamed of something greater—a government in which all people were equal.

## THE BIRTH OF A LEADER

On one particular night in the year 356 B.C.—the exact date is unknown—the sky over Ephesus in Asia Minor suddenly became a sea of light. The Temple of Artemis (Diana), one of the seven wonders of the world, was on fire. A man called Herostratus had set it aflame so that his name would be remembered in history. Angered by this deed, the citizens of Ephesus condemned Herostratus to death. They believed that the destruction of the temple was a sign that the seeds of the ruin of Asia had been planted that night.

On that very night in Pella, capital of Macedonia, Queen Olympias gave birth

Right: Alexander the Great as a young man. This statue, dating from the 2nd century B.C., is now in a museum in Istanbul, Turkey.
Below: The Temple of Apollo, on the heights of Delphi, Greece, as it appears today. From this temple the priestess Pythia foretold all of Alexander's victories in battle.

to a son. He was to be Alexander III, later known as Alexander the Great.

His father was King Philip II of Macedonia. Philip built a powerful army and conquered Greece. Occupied with military matters, he had little time for his son. The boy's education was left to his mother.

## A KINGDOM FOR A PRINCE

Most of Alexander's boyhood was spent in hunting and in sports. Plutarch, the Greek historian, tells us that when Alexander was about 12 years old, he succeeded in breaking a colt named Bucephalus. This colt had thrown all of King Philip's most able horsemen. Philip, who witnessed the event, embraced his son and said, "Look for a kingdom worthy of you, my son. Macedonia is too small for you!"

When he was 13 years old, Alexander began studying with Aristotle, one of the greatest scholars of all times. Aristotle made him aware of the existence of the human soul. He strengthened the sense of honor and dignity that Alexander had already acquired, mainly through reading the works of the Greek poet Homer. He had learned Homer's *Iliad* by heart because he thought it was the greatest textbook on military arts. He even kept a copy of it under his pillow.

What dreams of glory were Alexander's! The realization of these dreams was closer than he ever imagined. His father died when he was only 20. Rivals for the throne threatened him and tried to take his life. The Greek cities rebelled, and to the north the tribes of Thrace and the Illyrians led daring raids against him.

Fortunately, Alexander could depend upon the loyalty of the army that had admired him 2 years earlier during the battle of Chaeronea. At that time he had led the Macedonian cavalry charge that defeated Thebes. Winning this battle enabled Macedonia to dominate all of Greece.

*Alexander permitted only the painter Apelles and the sculptor Lysippus to reproduce his likeness. This copy of a statue by Lysippus was found in the excavations of Herculaneum in Italy. It is now in the National Museum in Naples.*

In 335 B.C., Alexander moved against the rebels with thousands of foot soldiers and horsemen. He marched at night, and with lightning speed he attacked the various Greek city-states. He forgave all of them except Thebes, which he destroyed almost completely.

The war in the north against the Thracians and Illyrians was difficult. The land was mountainous, making it easier for the poorly armed people to defend themselves. Yet time after time Alexander found ways to defeat them.

By 334 B.C. Alexander was victorious over what are now parts of Bulgaria, Greece, Rumania, and Yugoslavia. He then gathered his army on the banks of the Hellespont (Dardanelles)—the strait separating his realm from Asia Minor. The great adventure was about to begin!

Across the strait was the immense, powerful, and fabulously rich Persian Empire. It stretched 2,700 miles to the east, from western Asia Minor to the Punjab (now part of India and Pakistan). It also included northern Africa. Twice during the previous centuries the Persians had invaded Greece, sacking Athens and burning its holy Acropolis—the fortified hill overlooking the city. It was now Alexander's turn to carry out his father's plan and seek revenge on the Persian world.

His army set sail in 160 triremes—galleys having three banks of oars. When they landed on the other side of the strait Alexander hurled a javelin from the top deck of the royal trireme to the shore, declaring that he was taking possession of that land. He then set off for the ruins of Troy, where he placed his arms at the foot of the altar of the goddess Athena.

That same evening he called his friends together and divided his belongings among them. When one of them asked why he kept nothing for himself, he replied, "For myself, I keep only hope." His hope was great indeed, for although his army was well trained, it was far smaller than that of the Persians. Also, Alexander had no money and his army had to pay for itself as it went along. Persia, on the other hand, had immense resources. Alexander's challenge was like that of a flea against an elephant. When Persia's King Darius III was told that a youth not much more than 20 years old had dared war against him, he declared that Alexander had the rashness of a madman. Darius immediately dispatched a very large army to meet the enemy.

*Alexander and his horse Bucephalus in a painting by the Italian artist Tiepolo. When Bucephalus died after years of faithful service, his master founded a city in Asia to honor his memory.*

## THE GREAT ADVENTURE

This was to be Alexander's trial by fire. He was staking all he had. Victory meant conquest of Asia, but defeat meant the end of his dream, perhaps forever.

The Greek and Persian armies met on the banks of the Granicus River near Troy. The battle was an overwhelming victory for the Macedonians, who lost only 115 men. The Persians fled in disorder, losing 20,000 men. At least, that's the story that has come down to us, and the numbers may not be accurate.

Alexander continued his southward march around the Mediterranean, turning inland toward the Phrygian highlands. He spent the next winter at Gordium, capital of Phrygia. According to a legend of Gordium, anyone who succeeded in undoing the Gordian knot, which was tied to an ancient war chariot, would become master of all Asia. One story is that Alexander cut the knot with one bold blow of his sword. Another version states that he undid the knot by pulling out the pin that held it.

Regardless of which version is correct, Alexander had first to deal with Darius before the legend could come true. Alexander planned to capture the bases of the Persian fleet in the Mediterranean. Darius and a vast army moved to the area to meet him. In 333 B.C. the two armies met in a narrow valley in Issus (modern Turkey). Alexander's cavalry charge was so fierce that Darius fled. This caused his army to lose courage. Darius left behind him not only his wife and children, but also great riches. Alexander treated Darius' family with great kindness.

## TRIAL BY FIRE

After this victory Alexander marched against the Phoenician port cities and Palestine. Most surrendered without a fight. Tyre, however, held out for a time. Alexander continued on to Egypt where he was hailed as pharaoh (ruler). There he founded the city of Alexandria as a trade and cultural center. He also visited

*For over 8 years Alexander led his Macedonian soldiers in battles that made him master of much of the ancient world. He had conquered vast territories and founded 12 cities. He entered northern India and hoped to continue southward adding still more lands to his great empire. But he finally met with resistance from his own men. Weary from so many conquests, worn out by disease, hunger, and thirst, the soldiers rebelled and refused to go on. In 326 B.C. Alexander's armies began to prepare for the long journey home. The forces were divided into three groups: one under Craterus, one under Nearchus, an admiral, and one under Alexander himself. In 323 B.C. Alexander and his men reached Babylon, where Alexander hoped to build a fleet to sail around Arabia. But the great general was unable to carry out his plans. Weak and weary from his efforts, he fell ill and died. He was not quite 33 years old. His body, wrapped in golden cloth and placed in a glass coffin, was buried in Alexandria. Alexander's empire lasted only a short*

the famous Ammon (Zeus) oracle at the oasis of Siwa. There, the chief high priest greeted Alexander as a son. The priest's mispronunciation of a Greek word gave rise to the story that he had hailed Alexander as the "son of Zeus." Zeus was the greatest of the Greek gods.

Alexander then continued his campaign against Darius, who was defeated for the third time on the plains near Gaugamela, Mesopotamia, in 331 B.C. Alexander pursued the fleeing Darius, conquering many cities along the way. He took Babylon, Susa, Persepolis (where he burned the great palace of the kings), and Ecbatana (now Hamadan, Iran). In 330 B.C., at the Caspian Sea, he learned that Darius had been assassinated.

## A LEGEND FOR THE AGES

With the death of Darius, the Greek mission of revenge against the Persians was ended. But Alexander would not stop. He pushed forward to the Jaxartes River (modern Syr Darya), the northern limit of the Persian Empire. He then marched southeast across the dangerous passes of the Hindu Kush to the Punjab, the Land of the Five Rivers.

while after his death. The territory he had conquered was divided among his generals who soon began to quarrel among themselves. Finally, the empire broke up into many small independent regions, and Alexander's dream of a united kingdom came to an end. However, he had succeeded in spreading Greek culture to the countries under his rule, and Greek ideas lived on long after the empire had collapsed. Perhaps Alexander's greatest feat was the founding of the city of Alexandria, for hundreds of years a famous center of learning. One of his generals, Ptolemy I, became pharaoh of Egypt and did much to increase the capital's importance. Ptolemy founded Alexandria's famous library in which were placed all the works of the great authors of Greek literature. Among the scholars who studied there were the mathematician Euclid, the geographer Eratosthenes, and the scientist Herophilus who founded a medical school. Because of its natural harbor and sheltered port, Alexandria was also the great trading center for ships passing through the Mediterranean.

The Punjab was the eastern end of the Persian Empire. Here, at Hydaspes, Alexander fought his last great battle. It was against the Indian leader Porus. The horses of the Macedonians were frightened by the huge, armored elephants. Still, Alexander won. He wanted to go even farther east, but his army refused to follow. In 326 B.C. Alexander began his return march across the Gedrosia desert. While he was preparing a new expedition to explore the Arabian Peninsula, he became ill with a violent fever. He died in Babylon in June, 323 B.C., when he was not quite 33 years old.

It is not surprising that fanciful legends arose about Alexander. He became a god in Egyptian fables and a hero-saint to the Arabs. In France during the Middle Ages, he was a hero of tales of chivalry. Germans of the same time saw him as a kind of folk hero who carried his conquests to the very gate of paradise.

Alexander had a great goal—a one-world empire in which the various peoples were not only equal but joined by a common culture and commerce. His trade network and introduction of Greek culture to the East had a tremendous effect on future history.

# AN EMPEROR AND HIS EMPIRE

Like Alexander, Gaius Julius Caesar was of noble ancestry. He was born on July 12, 100 B.C., into the aristocratic Julian clan. Despite his ancestry Caesar supported the cause of the common people. This was partly due to the influence of his uncle Gaius Marius, leader of the democratic popular party. His association with Marius earned him the hatred of the nobles in the senate. This ill will made Caesar leave Rome to safeguard his life.

Caesar was able to return home in 78 B.C. He began a career in the law courts. His first important political post did not come until 69 B.C., when he was elected quaestor—a treasurer and collector of revenues—for Spain. Other offices followed, and it was while he was in charge of

*Left: A statue of Julius Caesar, the statesman-general who became supreme ruler of ancient Rome in 45 B.C.*
*Above: Copy of an ancient chariot. After a victorious battle, the Roman armies marched through the streets of the city. Caesar rode at their head in a chariot like the one pictured.*
*Right: Caesar was one of Rome's most brilliant generals. He was also a gifted orator and writer. His accounts of his battles, still widely read, are known for their clear, direct style.*

public games that he became popular with the public. After being governor of Spain (61 B.C.), Caesar formed an alliance with Pompey and Crassus, the most powerful men in Rome. With their support he became a leader of the Roman Republic in 59 B.C.

Caesar next sought military fame. Between 58 and 51 B.C. he defeated the tribes of Gaul, from northern Italy to the Rhine River. He invaded Britain twice. The nobles grew more fearful of him and demanded that he stop fighting and return to Rome. Caesar agreed but only if Pompey, who had begun to side with the nobles, did likewise. Pompey refused and in January of 49 B.C. Caesar and his army crossed the Rubicon and returned to Italy. It was then he is supposed to have said "The die is cast."

Within 6 weeks Caesar ruled Italy. He pursued Pompey to Greece and to Egypt, where Pompey was murdered. Caesar made Cleopatra ruler of Egypt and went to Asia Minor to calm a revolt. When he defeated its leader, Pharnaces, in a very short time, Caesar said "*Veni, vidi, vici*" ("I came, I saw, I conquered.")

During the following years Caesar began to reorganize Rome. He extended Roman citizenship to non-Romans and he improved the calendar. Many Romans feared that he planned to become king and plotted his death. On the Ides (15th) of March, 44 B.C., Caesar died under their daggers. His conquests stopped the barbarian invasions from the north and east for centuries. They also led to the spread of Greco-Roman ideas to what is now Europe.

## THE PAST IS UNLOCKED

One moment, please. I just realized that I have been mentioning great cities of the past, such as Troy and Babylon. You may not know it but until recently many of these cities were thought of as purely imaginary or as having vanished long ago without trace. In the 18th and 19th centuries men who could be called explorers began to search for them. To the world's surprise, they found the remains of these and other cities buried beneath the earth. Pluto is shaking his head. The only discoveries in the earth he's interested in are bones!

Much of what we know about the ancient peoples who lived in these cities comes from their own writings. Since their ways of writing were not like ours, we could not read them for a long time. For example, scholars had known about Egyptian hieroglyphics—writing by means of pictorial characters—for cen-

*Left: Gold mask of Tutankhamen, pharaoh of Egypt, who reigned around the middle of the 14th century B.C.
Right: Terra-cotta jars were filled with offerings to the gods. Those shown here were found at Sakkara, a burying ground near Memphis, capital of the Old Kingdom of ancient Egypt.*

turies. No one knew what the pictorial characters meant until the Rosetta Stone was found by one of the engineers Napoleon Bonaparte took on his campaign to Egypt in 1798. On the stone there was writing in Greek as well as hieroglyphics and another form of ancient Egyptian writing. By comparing them, scholars were finally able to decipher hieroglyphics.

## DIGGING FOR HISTORY

From his early youth the German Heinrich Schliemann (1822–90) loved the poems of Homer. He even dreamed of finding Troy, the great city of King Priam. Schliemann made a fortune in the import business and retired at an early age to travel and study the culture of ancient Greece. He was determined to find Troy, although most experts thought it existed only in the pages of Homer's *Iliad*. In 1871 Schliemann began to dig in a hill near Hissarlik, in northwestern Turkey. He discovered that there were layers under the earth and that each one contained the remains of a different settlement. There were nine in all, and Troy was the seventh stratum, or layer.

Opposite page: Uxmal, on the Yucatan Peninsula in Mexico, was abandoned by the Maya Indians more than 300 years ago. The American archeologist John Lloyd Stephens discovered the city in the last century.
Above: The Valley of the Kings in Egypt, where archeologists discovered many treasures. The tomb of Tutankhamen was unearthed here in 1922.

The Englishman Sir Arthur Evans (1851–1941) grew up with people who loved history and cultures of the past. He became interested in the ancient civilizations of Greece, especially Crete, which he believed was one of the earliest centers of Greek culture. He noticed that many young women in Greece wore a strange engraved stone around their necks as charms. Evans believed the symbols on them were samples of early Cretan writing. While searching for more of these stones on Crete, he found piles of ruins. He began to dig there in 1899. Within a week the outlines of Knossos, the greatest of Cretan cities, became visible. He found the palace of King Minos with its labyrinths—the twisting paths in which the legendary Minotaur (half-bull and half-man) was supposed to have roamed.

*Heinrich Schliemann, son of a poor German pastor, grew up on tales of ancient Greek heroes. His imagination was fired by the stories of the Trojan War as told by the Greek poet Homer. As a young man, Schliemann worked hard to earn enough money to pay for archeological expeditions to Asia Minor, site of the war Homer described. His purpose was to prove that Troy had been a real city and that Homer's stories were true. He led excavations from 1871–1882. On the hill of Hissarlik in modern Turkey, he uncovered the ruins of the ancient city that, through the centuries, had been destroyed and rebuilt nine times. Right, above: A simplified diagram of the layers of ancient Troy. Right, below: The south gate of Troy as it appears today.*

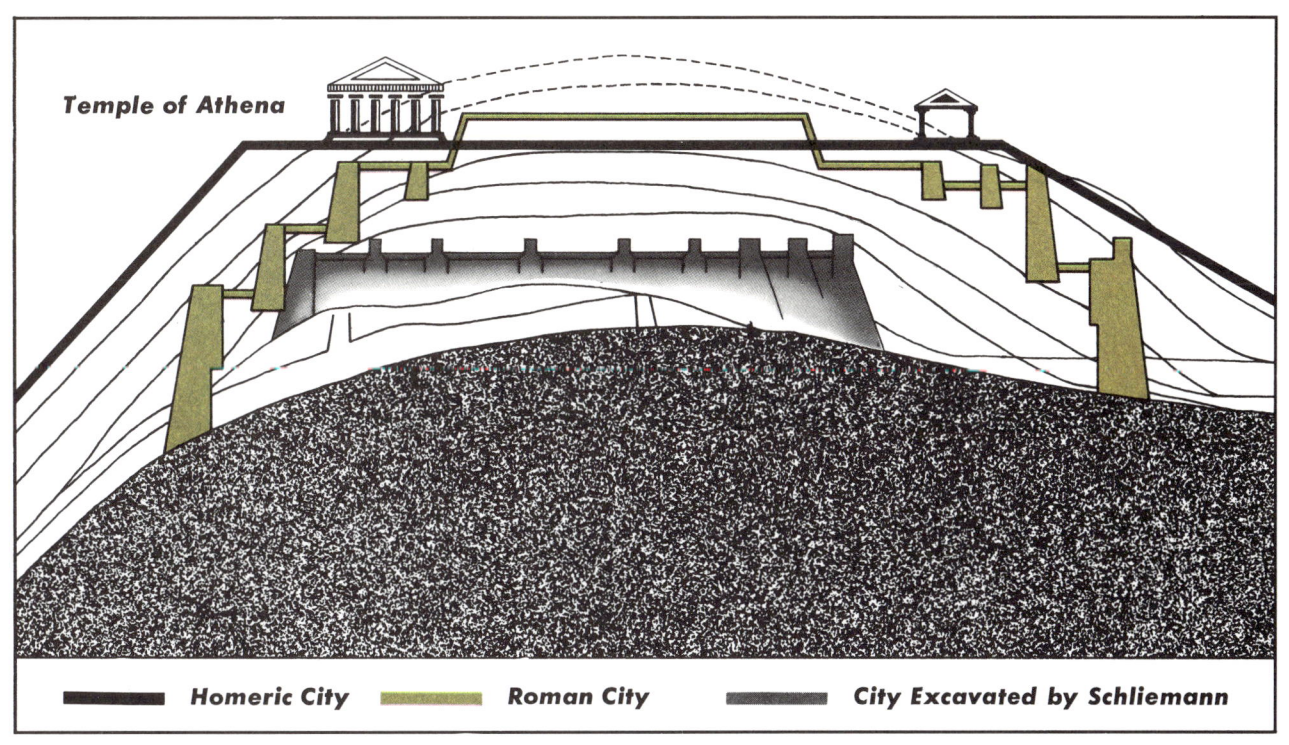

Temple of Athena
Homeric City
Roman City
City Excavated by Schliemann

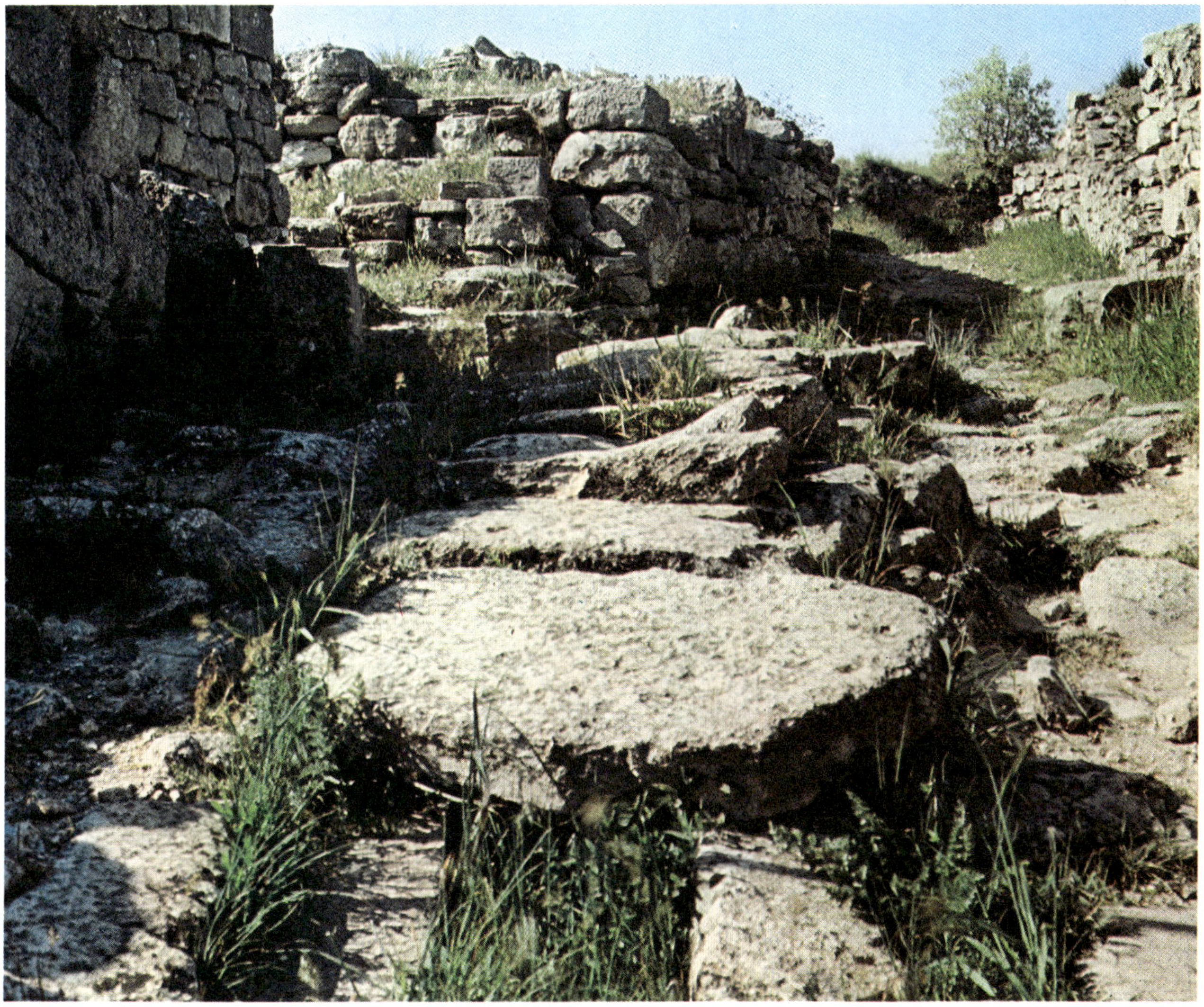

# THE CITY OF A THOUSAND COLUMNS

Not all great cities of legend were found in Europe and Asia. Nor were they all built in the centuries before Christ. The Maya and Aztec Indians of Central and South America, for example, built a number of great cities between the 4th and 15th centuries.

Toward the middle of the 17th century, a researcher in Madrid discovered a report written about 100 years earlier by the Franciscan bishop Diego de Landa. The report told of the Mayan cities of the Yucatan Peninsula in Mexico. The Spaniards had never heard of the cities it described, such as Chichén Itzá, and did not believe the report. Two centuries later the American Edward Thompson (1860?-1935), spurred on by his faith in the report, set out for the jungles of Yucatan. Above all, he wanted to discover the sacred well into which the ancient Mayans had thrown young girls, warriors, and jewels. These were offerings to the rain gods called Chacs, whom the people believed lived in the bottom of the well.

Finding the city proved difficult for Thompson because he had only the manuscript and a native to guide him, and because thick undergrowth blocked the way. At long last, on a bright moonlit night, he

*Above:* The pyramid of El Tajín near Papantla, Mexico.
*Right:* El Castillo (The Castle) in Chichén Itzá, on the Yucatan Peninsula in Mexico. Chichén Itzá, an ancient Mayan Indian city, was abandoned late in the 15th century. This structure, named by the Spanish conquerors, was probably used by Mayan priests for performing religious sacrifices.

came out of the jungle in the center of the Mayan capital—Chichén Itzá, the city of the Thousand Columns.

The fabulous well was found, and Thompson later went down into it with a diving suit. He discovered the remains of the offerings and the sacrifices. He also found several buildings and an immense platform that supported a great pyramid, temples, a ball-court, and the Court of the Thousand Columns, which had probably been a marketplace.

*Left: Statue of a Mayan god at an entrance to the Temple of the Warriors in Chichén Itzá.*
*Below: Carved stone serpents guard one of the entrances to the Temple of the Warriors.*

# EXPLORERS AND NAVIGATORS

What courage the early explorers must have had! Just think, boys and girls, those hardy adventurers had no maps to guide them, no compasses to point the way. They had only the sun, the moon, and the stars to tell direction by. I must admit that I would have been a poor explorer. When Minnie and I take a trip, I need a map and a compass to find the airport.

You might be wondering why the first explorers sailed off on dangerous voyages to unknown places. Some were simply curious about what they would find beyond the great oceans. Many went looking for gold and other riches. Others wanted to spread their religious beliefs. "Glory, Gold, and God" were the main reasons why men risked death on these great adventures.

40

# THE BOLD VIKINGS

You may have seen pictures of the Vikings, with their long beards and their helmets decorated with ox horns. I have one of those helmets here, and I'm going to wear it while I talk to you about the Vikings. More than 1,000 years ago, these fierce Norsemen (men of the North) raided and plundered towns and villages all along the coasts of Europe and North Africa. The word "viking" means pirate in the old Norse language—and the Vikings lived up to their name. They were known for their cruelty and love of fighting. Their enemies hated and feared them.

But the Vikings were also daring explorers. Their long and narrow sailing ships carried them from Norway,

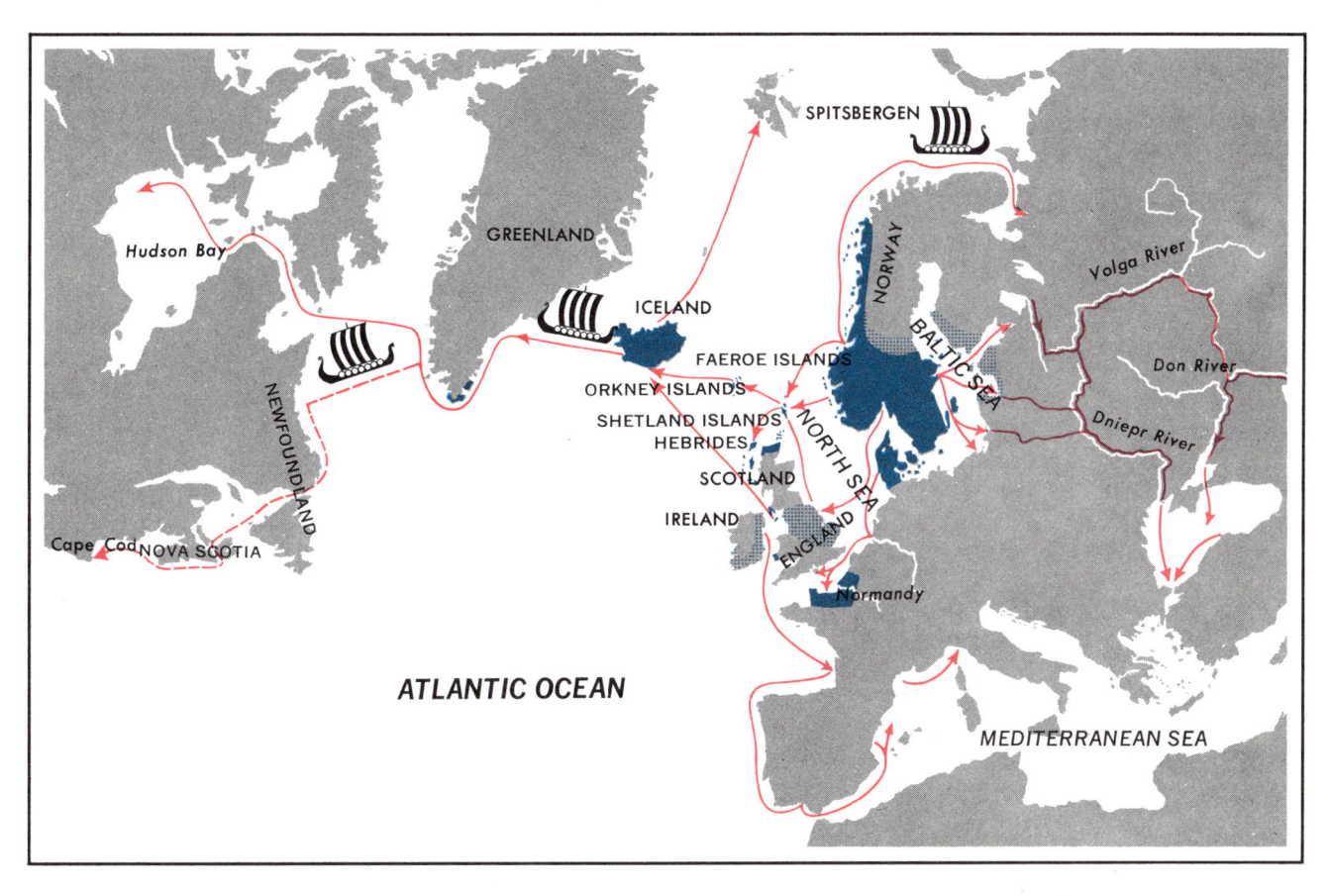

Left: Carved head of a sea serpent. Such figures decorated the prows of Viking funeral ships.
Above: The blue areas on the map show the lands occupied by the Vikings. The red lines show the routes of their explorations. Viking seafarers explored as far west as North America.

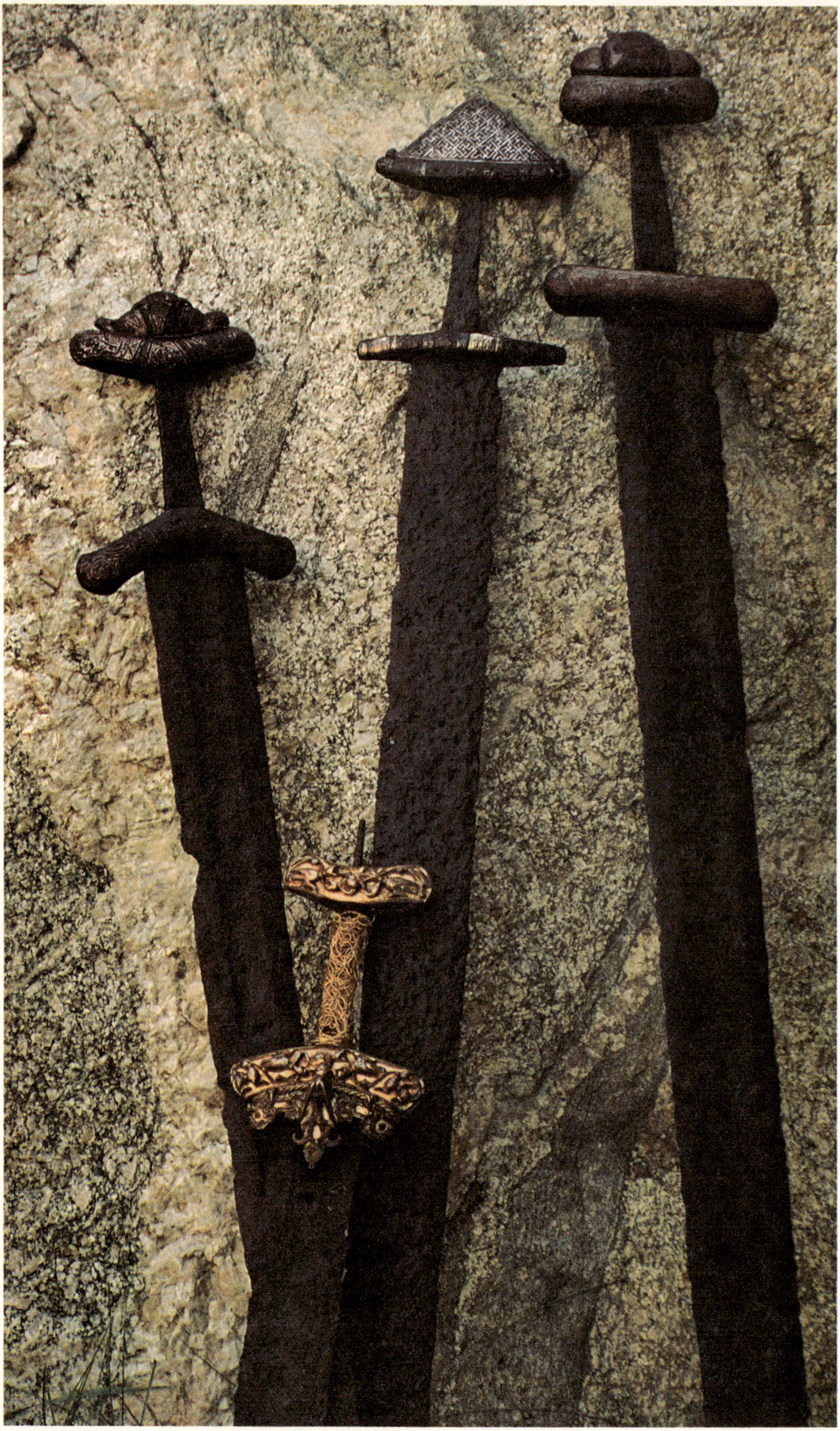

Sweden, and Denmark, their homelands, to the shores of Greenland and North America. The Vikings had a clever way of navigating (setting a course) when they went exploring. They took ravens (crow-like birds) with them and released one of the birds every few days. At first the ravens flew back to the land from which the ship had come. On and on the ship moved and one day the raven would fly in another direction. The Vikings followed the raven's course, knowing that they were approaching land—new land.

*Opposite page: Viking swords in Stockholm's Museum of National Antiquities. The shortest may have been made by someone trained in Britain.*
*Above: Viking warriors' helmets from the same museum. They were found in the tombs of Vendel in Uppland, where the remains of Viking funeral ships were unearthed. The Viking custom of burying their chiefs in funeral ships lasted for centuries. When the burial mounds were found, the wooden ships had rotted away. But the metal objects buried with the chiefs were often perfectly preserved.*

# THE VIKINGS DISCOVER AMERICA

Among the famous Viking explorers was a man who was nicknamed Eric the Red because of his red hair and beard. Eric grew up in Iceland, where his father had been sent as punishment for having killed another Viking. Eric had a terrible temper, and one day he killed one of his neighbors in a fight. The Vikings declared him an outlaw and ordered him to leave Iceland for 3 years.

Eric, his family, and friends loaded their possessions on board 25 ships and sailed away. Other Vikings told them about a large island to the west, so they headed in that direction. Eventually they landed on the rugged coast of this island. Although it was mostly icy wasteland, Eric called it Greenland. He hoped the name would attract settlers, which it did.

A Viking settlement was started around A.D. 985. It lasted for about 400 years.

Eric had a son who was named Leif Ericson—also known as Leif the Lucky. Leif, too, was an explorer. Around the year 1000, Leif and his crew were caught in a storm while sailing from Norway to Greenland. For many days they were lost at sea. At last they sighted land—the coast of North America.

No one is sure where Leif and his men first came ashore. It may have been as far north as Labrador in present-day Canada or as far south as Virginia. The Vikings described the place as being covered by vast forests, wheat fields, and grapevines. They called it Vinland, or Wineland. Other expeditions followed and settlements were built. However, the Indians later drove out the Vikings. But the fact remains, boys and girls, that the Vikings discovered America 500 years before Columbus.

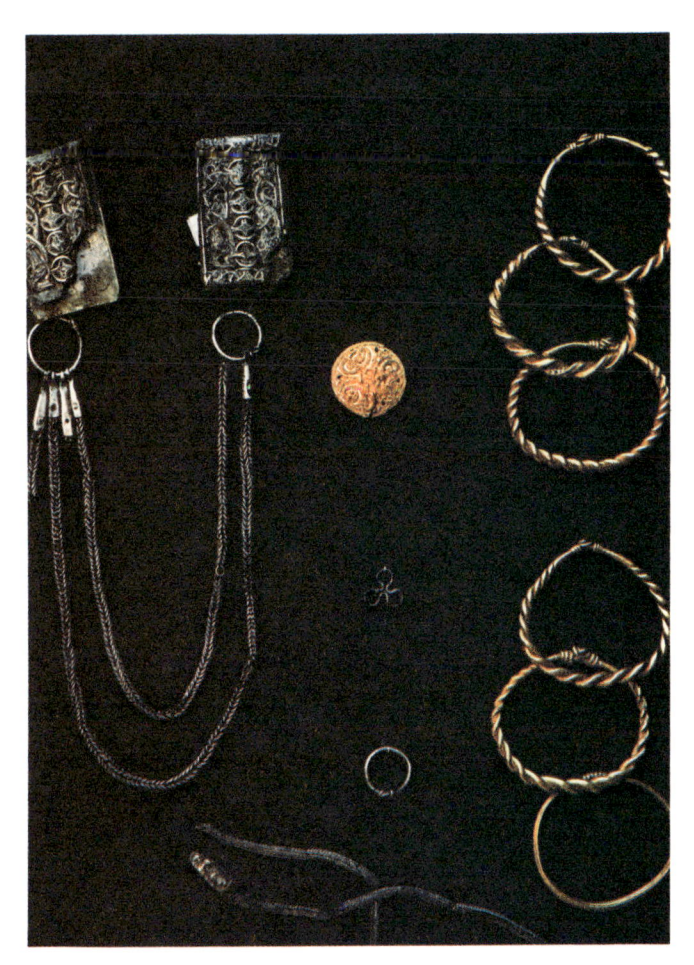

Upper left: Necklaces, bracelets, and other ornaments from the second half of the 10th century.
Lower left: Graduated scale used for weighing, from the 11th century.
Below: A tool from the Swedish island of Gotland, made in the year 1000.
Bottom: Carved gravestones found in central Sweden.

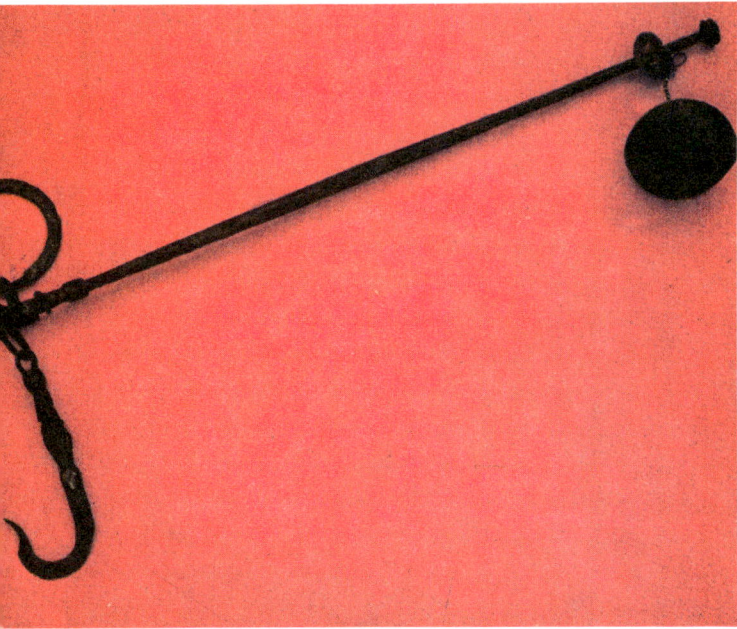

Opposite page, left: A Viking hut in Denmark's Jutland peninsula. The wood-and-turf hut was preserved by being deeply buried by a landslide of sand. Jutland also has well-preserved burial mounds. Opposite page, right: A Viking ornament made of gold.

# MARCO POLO

Have you ever heard of Marco Polo, my young friends? No, it has nothing to do with the game of polo! Marco Polo was an Italian merchant who became famous for his travels to China and the farthest reaches of Asia. Actually, he wasn't an explorer like Leif Ericson or Christopher Columbus. Nor was he even the first European to visit China. But he was the first Westerner to journey across the whole breadth of Asia—from Persia (now Iran) to the islands of Indonesia. And he was the first to describe in detail the different Asian kingdoms and peoples, with their strange ways and customs.

Marco Polo was born in Venice, a city on the east coast of Italy, in the year 1254. His father Niccolo and his uncle Maffeo Polo were both merchants. They had traveled to the heart of Asia and the court of the Chinese emperor Kubla Khan to buy jewels, spices, and silk. Oh my, I better not speak too loudly about jewels with Uncle Scrooge nearby.

*Marco Polo (1254–1324), greatest traveler of the Middle Ages. His descriptions of his travels influenced early map makers. Born in Venice, Polo set out at 17 with his father and uncle on an adventure-filled journey to China.*

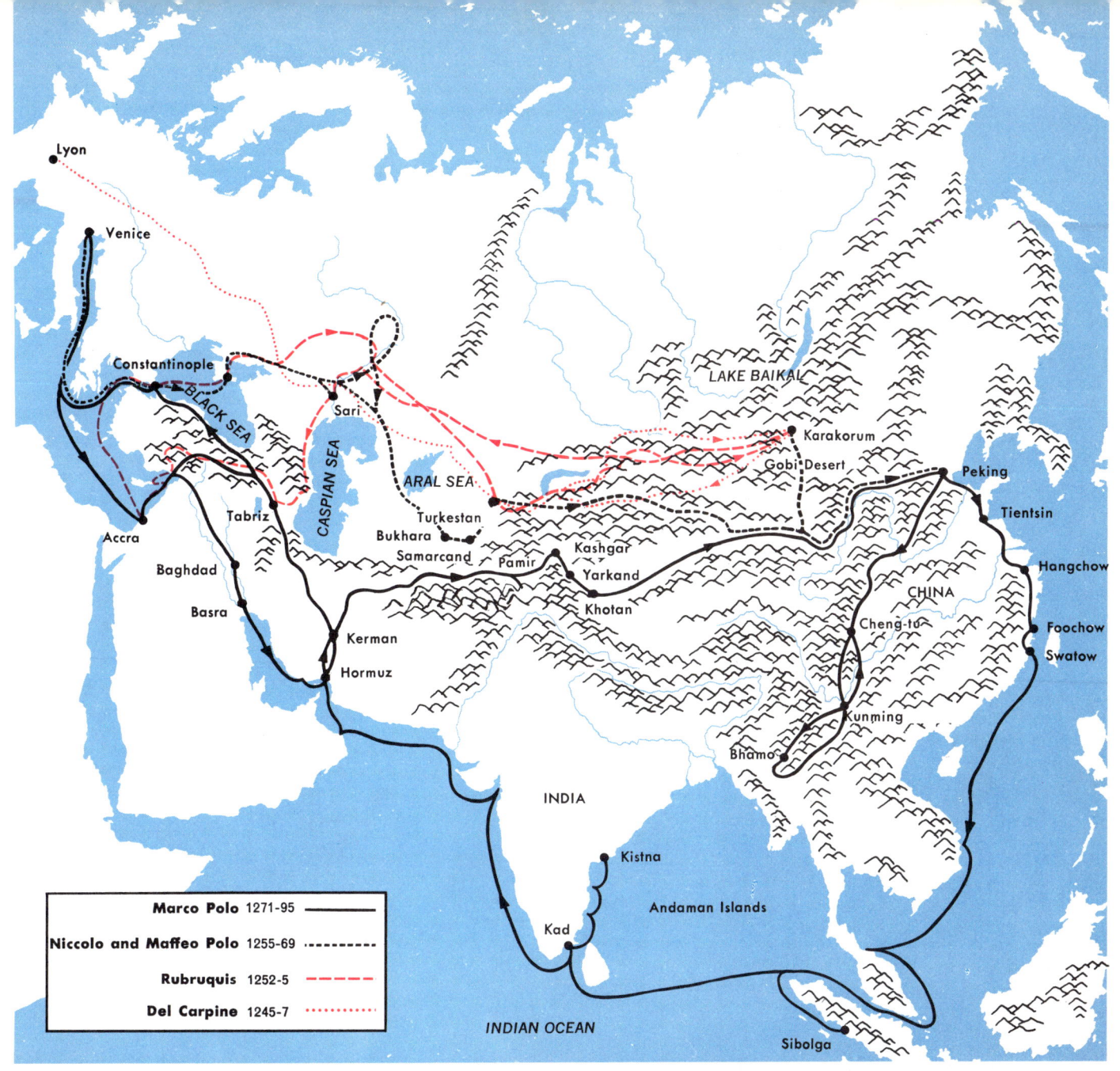

| Legend | Route |
|---|---|
| Marco Polo 1271-95 | ——— |
| Niccolo and Maffeo Polo 1255-69 | - - - - |
| Rubruquis 1252-5 | – – – |
| Del Carpine 1245-7 | ········ |

*Above: The routes traced on the map show that the Polos were not the first Europeans to travel to Asia. But they also show that Marco Polo and his father and uncle traveled the most widely. Marco Polo's fame rests on the detailed description he wrote of the people and places he visited during his journeys throughout the Mongol empire.*

*Right: Marco Polo dictating the story of his travels in a Genoa prison. In 1298, 3 years after he returned from Asia, war broke out between Venice and Genoa. Polo was captured by the Genoese and while in prison dictated the story of his 24 years in the Orient to his cellmate, Rusticiano of Pisa. The book was written in French on parchment.*

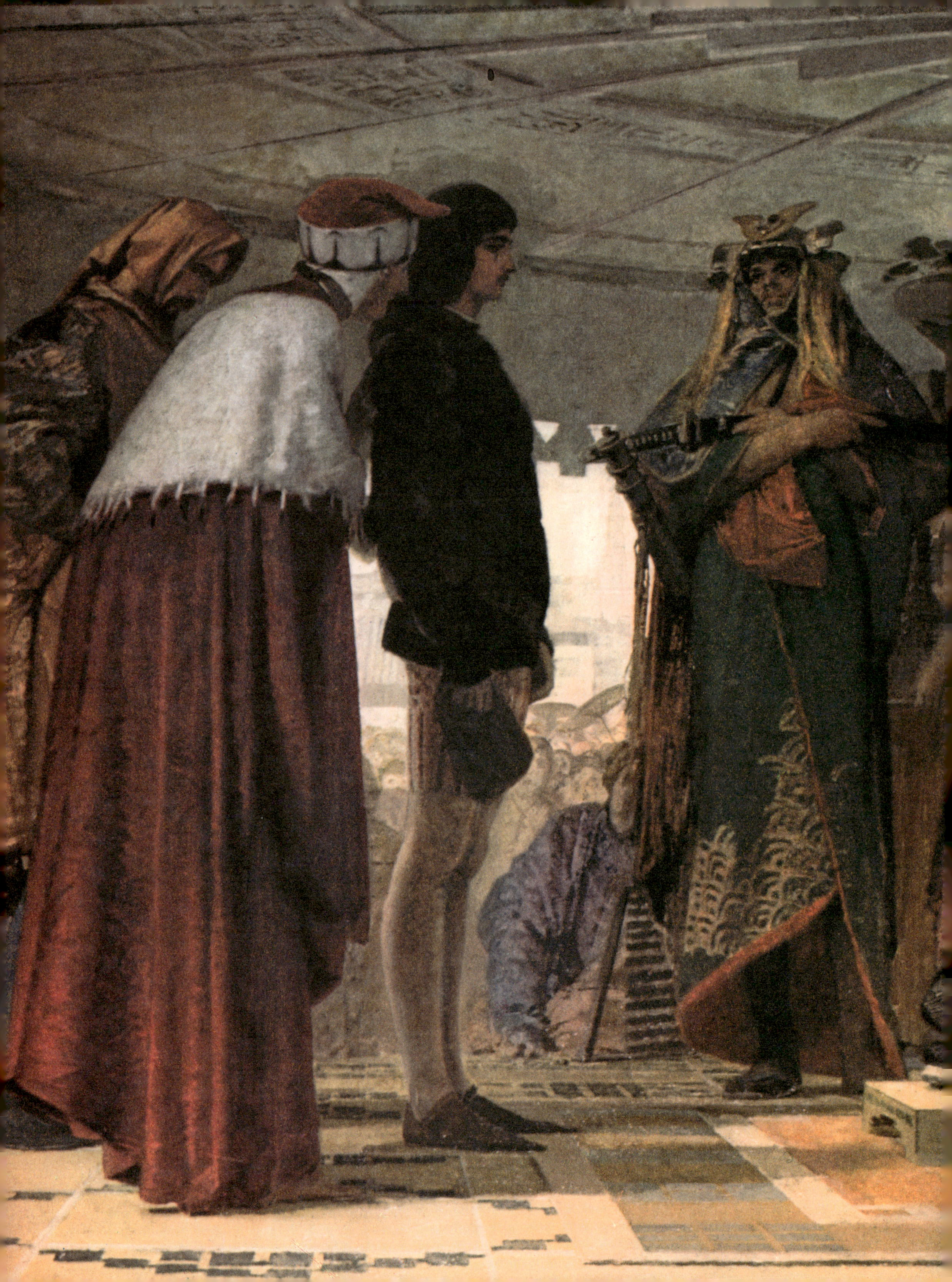

"*Who is this courageous lad?*" *asked the great Kubla Khan. Niccolo Polo replied, "He is my son!"* (*The painting is by Tranquillo Cremona.*)

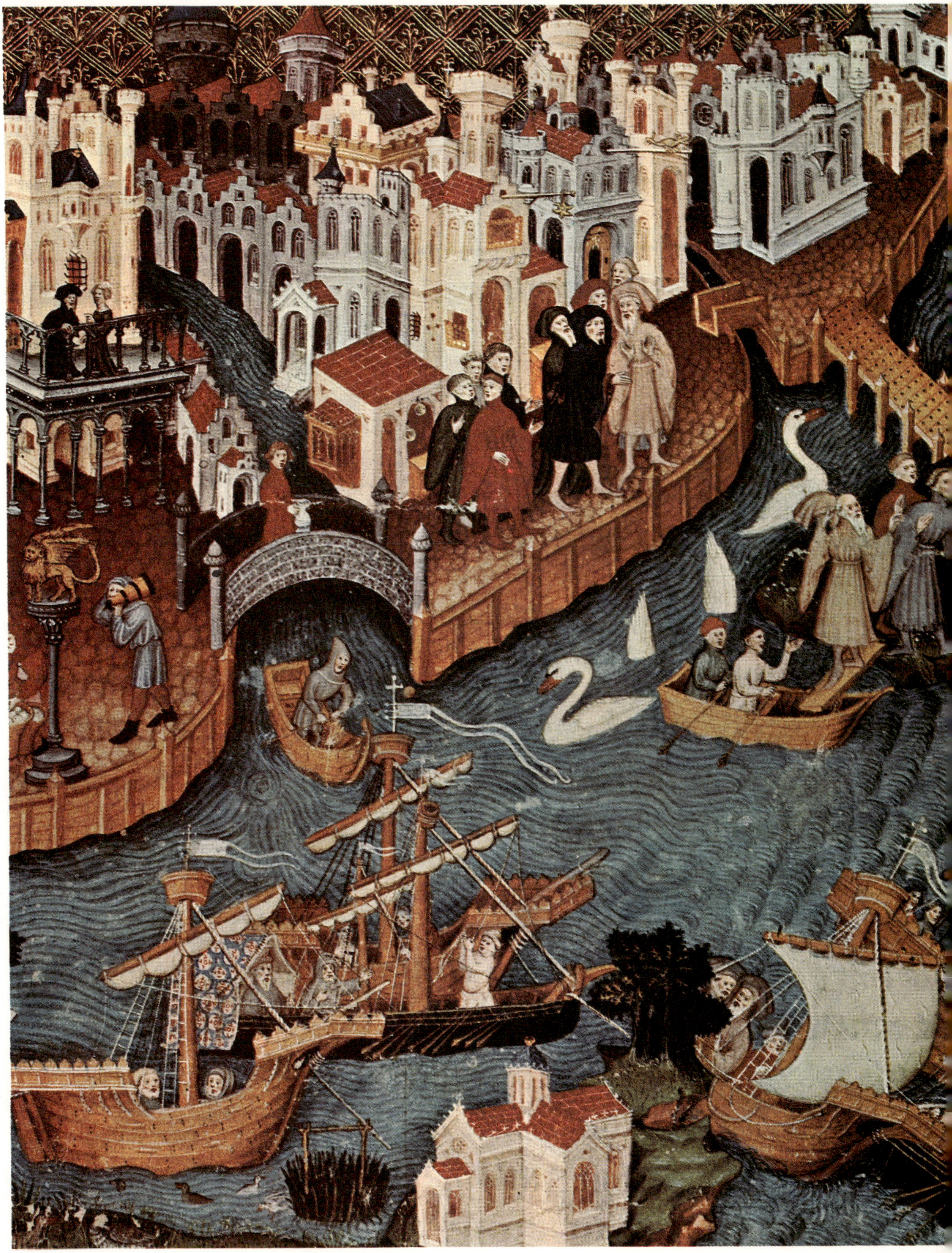

But never mind, let me continue with my story. Marco was a boy of 15 when his father and uncle returned to Venice. Kubla Khan had asked Maffeo and Niccolo to bring back 100 scholars to teach Western knowledge to the Chinese. These scholars were to be selected by the Pope. But the old Pope had died and the new one was busy with other matters. So after 2 years of delay, Marco, his father, and his uncle started on another long and difficult journey to Asia.

Today we can take a trip to Asia by plane in a matter of hours. (Of course my friend Pluto would have to fly in the baggage compartment.) But 700 years ago it took a much longer time. In fact, it took the Polos nearly 4 years. First they had to take a ship from Venice to Palestine. Next they traveled by camel across Arabia and Persia. They went through burning hot deserts and up into the highest mountains of Central Asia. Marco kept a full record of their adventures in his notebooks.

By following the ancient caravan route, they finally reached China and the palace of Kubla Khan. The great emperor was overjoyed to see them. He took an immediate liking to the intelligent, quick-witted Marco. The young man was used as a courier to carry important messages to Burma, Indochina, Malaya, and Indonesia. All the while Marco kept a written account of everything he saw.

After living in China for 17 years, the Polos wanted to return home. They got their chance when the Khan asked them to escort a young Chinese princess to his grand-nephew, the ruler of Persia. The Polos carried out their mission and then continued on to Venice. They arrived home in 1295. They had been gone for almost 25 years.

*The Polos return to Venice in 1295. They had been away so long that they were greatly changed. Their clothes were shabby and worn and their relatives had trouble recognizing them. Imagine the surprise of the Venetians when they found that the ragged clothes of the three travelers were stuffed with precious stones! It was by this clever trick that the Polos had avoided being attacked by bandits.*

Soon after their return, war broke out between Venice and Genoa, a rival city. Marco was captured and imprisoned. While in prison Marco dictated his story to a fellow captive, who was a writer. Marco told of the great cities of China and the broad highways and beautiful palaces he had seen. He also described paper money—Europeans still used heavy metal coins—and black stones that burned. Europeans had not yet heard about coal.

Many people thought Marco had made up a tall tale. They called him a liar and laughed at him. But the story of his adventures, which he called *The Book of Marco Polo*, was read by many people. It influenced map makers and explorers, including Christopher Columbus. Well now, I've mentioned Columbus several times, so why don't we turn to his story.

*Using Marco Polo's descriptions, the Venetian map maker Fra Mauro designed this map of the world in the mid-1400's. In the empty spaces Fra Mauro placed quotations from the book of Marco Polo. Because South is at the top on this map, you must turn this book upside down to see the continents as you are used to seeing them. Mauro's map is a masterpiece, and it was one of the sources Christopher Columbus later used in his geographical studies. It can be seen today in the Marciana Library in Venice.*

53

# THE ADMIRAL OF THE OCEAN SEA

I agree with the people who believe that the discovery of America was the single most courageous deed in the course of human history. But I disagree with those who say that Columbus wouldn't have set out on such a risky venture if he had known that it was based on a huge geographic error. I believe that even if Columbus had known that the world was much larger than most men thought, he would have done it anyway. That's what *I* think!

You see, during the Middle Ages most scholars believed that the circumference (distance around) of our planet was much smaller than it actually is.

What's that? You want to know how the scientists of that time could have made such a mistake? First I have to mention the Greek mathematician and geographer named Eratosthenes, who lived in the 3rd century B.C. He worked out a figure that was amazingly close to the actual circumference of the earth.

# THE STORY OF AN ERROR

Well, now I can tell you how their error came about. During the Middle Ages there was a great deal of trade between the Europeans and the Arabs. But besides goods and money, knowledge was also exchanged. The Europeans learned much of what they knew about the ancient world of Greece and Rome from the Arabs. This knowledge included Eratosthenes' figures for the circumference of the earth.

The Arabs had translated his measurements into miles from the older units called *stadia*. But their miles were about 20 percent longer than those used by the European map makers at the time. Because of this difference, the circumference of the earth was reduced by one fifth. A big difference!

Also, during the Middle Ages many men believed that when God created the world, he commanded all the waters to withdraw to the seventh part of the earth. This meant that our planet was six parts dry land. If only one seventh of the earth was occupied by water, then the oceans must really be quite small!

In the Italian city of Florence, a doctor and astronomer named Paolo dal Pozzo Toscanelli was studying the earth's geog-

*Below: The frontispiece of the "Book of Privileges," granted to Columbus by King Ferdinand and Queen Isabella.*
*Bottom right: The coat of arms granted to Columbus as Admiral of the Ocean Sea. At top are Isabella's emblems of Castile (a castle) and León (a lion). Beneath are a group of islands and several anchors, standing for discovery and seafaring.*

*Opposite page: Portrait of Columbus.*
*Above: Statue of Christopher Columbus as a boy in Genoa, Italy, his birthplace. Columbus is gazing thoughtfully at the sea. As sometimes happens with great historical figures, many cities claim Columbus. The Italian towns of Nervi, Cogoleto, Bogliasco, and Savona claim him and so do cities in France, Spain, Portugal, and England. But Columbus stated clearly in his will, "I drew my origins from the city of Genoa, where I was born." The Spanish consider him one of their own, and they call him Cristóbal Colón.*

raphy. He had also read Marco Polo's account of his travels. Toscanelli came to believe that Asia was much larger than most people thought. In 1474 he wrote that a voyage from Portugal to Japan could be made in a few days by sailing westward across the Atlantic. Ships could be resupplied at the island of Antillia, about one third of the way across. (The fact that there was no such island was not discovered until many years later.)

So the route was clearly marked. All that was needed was someone with the courage to follow it. That someone was Christopher Columbus. Of course, if I had been alive then, I'd have been glad to do the job myself!

Columbus was born in Genoa—a port city on Italy's northwest coast—in 1451. We don't have too many facts about his boyhood, but we do know that he first went to sea when he was quite young. Later he began to study map-making, and as he made more voyages, he became a skillful navigator. His ambition to find the shortest and safest sea route to the riches of the Indies (as the Far East was called in those days) started to grow.

Columbus exchanged letters with Toscanelli. Gradually he worked out his plan to reach the East by sailing west. In 1484 he presented this plan to King John II of Portugal. Portugal was one of the leading seafaring nations of Europe. The King

*Opposite page:* The port of Genoa as it looked in the time of Columbus.
*Above:* The famous Map of Christopher Columbus. *According to some historians, this map was drawn by Columbus himself.*

*Two artists' versions of Columbus' departure from Palos, Spain. Above: A 16th-century engraving showing Columbus saying farewell to Queen Isabella and King Ferdinand.
Opposite page: A painting in which a much older looking Columbus kisses the hand of Father Perez, who had helped persuade Queen Isabella to finance the expedition.*

turned the plan over to a committee of experts. They decided the project would fail, and so they turned it down.

But Columbus did not give up. He turned to Spain, Portugal's great rival as a sea power. The young Spanish monarchs—King Ferdinand II of Aragon and Queen Isabella of Castile—also gave the plan to a committee for study. Again, this time after 4 years of discussion, it was turned down. It really was difficult to discover America, wasn't it, boys and girls?

But Columbus kept trying. At long last, in 1492, Queen Isabella agreed to finance the project. The royal treasurer, Luis de Santangel, also contributed to it, and Columbus himself put up some of the money, which he probably borrowed.

If he succeeded in reaching the East, he was to receive the Spanish noble title of *don*. He would also become admiral and ruler of all the lands he discovered, and he would be entitled to one tenth of the gold, silver, gems, and spices found there.

I'm sure I don't have to tell you the names of the three ships that made the first voyage to the New World. But perhaps I can tell you a few things about the ships and the men who sailed in them that you may not know.

The flagship of the tiny fleet, the *Santa María*, was commanded by Columbus himself. She was nicknamed the *Capitana* and carried a crew of 40 men. The two other ships were smaller, both of the kind called caravels. The one we know as the *Niña* was actually named the *Santa Clara*. She was nicknamed for her owners, the Nino family of Moguer, Spain. The *Niña* had a crew of 24. Her captain was Vincente Yáñez Pinzón, a member of a seafaring family. His brother, Martin Alonzo Pinzón, commanded the *Pinta*, with a 26-man crew.

Except for four of the crewmen—and of course Columbus himself—all of the men who made the voyage were Spaniards.

# AUGUST 3, 1492

About half an hour before sunrise on August 3, 1492, Columbus' fleet set sail from Palos, on Spain's southwest coast.

The little fleet reached the Canary Islands, some 700 miles to the southwest, on August 12. There they stopped for almost a month. The *Pinta's* rudder needed repairs, and the *Niña's* sails were changed. She had originally carried the great triangular sails typical of most caravels. Columbus decided that if the *Niña's* rigging were converted to square sails, she would ride the waves more steadily and more safely. The three ships also took on fresh supplies in the Canaries.

Finally, on September 6, the *Santa María*, the *Pinta*, and the *Niña* weighed anchor and set sail from the Canaries. They were leaving behind them the Old World and everything familiar. They were venturing out into an ocean that was known only through legends and superstitions. Some of these tales told of boiling waters, strange calms, monsters who lived in the depths, and other things nobody could explain.

After about a week, the compass began to behave strangely. Instead of pointing north, it pointed slightly to the west. The men became terrified, for without a working compass, they might all be lost. Columbus explained that their location had affected the compass reading, and that they were still on course. The voyage continued.

Columbus knew that his crewmen would grow more frightened the farther they sailed. So he decided to record in the daily ship's log less mileage than was actually covered. However, he did keep the correct figures in a secret log.

But in spite of this, the men became more restless with every passing day. All around, as far as the eye could see, were the sea and the sky. There was danger of mutiny. Many of the sailors grumbled that if Columbus was right, they should have reached Asia long before.

At long last, before dawn on October 12, 1492, the lookout on the *Pinta* sighted land. They had reached the Bahama Islands, east of Florida. Although they believed it was Asia, they had found the New World!

*Painting by Niccolo Barabino showing the monks at the University of Salamanca laughing at Columbus and his plans to sail west to Asia. Experts at the Spanish university had examined Columbus' project for 4 years and then turned it down. They though the idea half-mad.*

61

The little island on which they landed was called Guanahani by the natives. (Today it is usually called Watling Island.) Columbus named it San Salvador, and he took possession of it for King Ferdinand and Queen Isabella.

The people of San Salvador wore no clothes, and many of them painted their bodies in bright colors. They were friendly and glad to share their food and whatever they had with Columbus and his men. But although some of them wore small gold ornaments, they had no source of gold. So, several days later, the three ships sailed on, still searching for Japan.

After stopping at various other islands in the Bahamas, the fleet reached Cuba on October 28. Columbus had taken along several Indians from San Salvador. They would serve as guides, enabling him and his men to find gold more quickly.

But in spite of the guides, a misunderstanding soon developed. When Columbus asked the Cuban natives where he could find gold, they replied with the word *Cubanacan*, or "In the middle of Cuba." But Columbus thought they said "the Grand Khan." This was the title of the emperor of China whom Marco Polo had written about. So Columbus sent a group of men as official ambassadors to greet the powerful Chinese ruler. The head of the party, Luis de Torres, was chosen because he knew Hebrew and Arabic. No Europeans at that time knew Chinese, and perhaps they thought it would be similar to the Middle Eastern languages.

Torres and his group returned without having found the Grand Khan or the gold, and the fleet sailed again. On December 6 they reached Haiti, which Columbus named Hispaniola. Here again the natives had gold, but Columbus and his men never learned where it came from. On Christmas Eve the *Santa María* ran

*Opposite page: Reproductions of two caravels represent the fleet of Christopher Columbus sailing into a bay in the New World.*

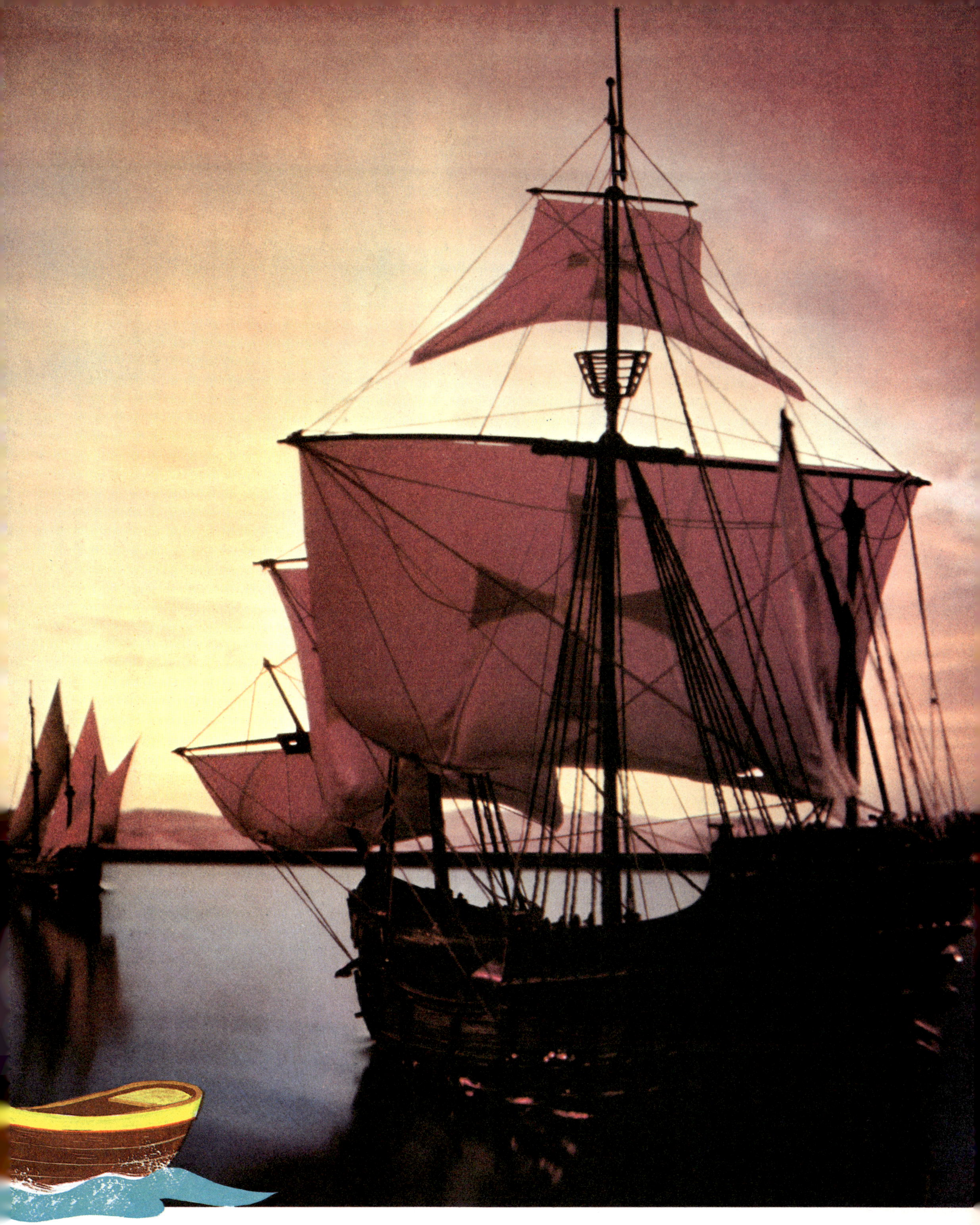

*Left: A display of equipment for the masts and sails of a ship in the time of Columbus.*
*Opposite page, above: Routes of Columbus' four voyages to the New World.*
*Opposite page, below: A print of Amerigo Vespucci (1451–1512), who helped outfit ships for Columbus' second and third voyages of discovery. Later Vespucci himself made voyages of exploration, becoming a map maker and pilot. During some of these voyages, he landed on the coasts of South America. He realized that the lands discovered by Columbus were not part of Asia but were actually a "new world." In 1507 the map maker Martin Waldseemüller suggested the new continent be named "Amerige" or "America" in honor of the man who first distinguished it from Asia. At first the name was given only to South America. Later it was used for North America as well.*

aground in a bay on the northern coast of Haiti, and it was impossible to float her again. Columbus left her crew of 40 with instructions to build a colony there, which he called *La Navidad* (Spanish for "Christmas"). The *Pinta* had become separated from the other ships about 3 months earlier and only rejoined them now. On January 4, 1493, Columbus set sail for Spain in the *Niña*.

The voyage home was a rough one, and Columbus did not reach Spain until March 15. He was received by the King and Queen a month later. He gave them the birds, plants, and the six Indians he had brought back with him as well as what little gold he had obtained.

The monarchs were pleased with Columbus' gifts and with his tales of discovery. A second voyage was planned. This time Columbus was given a free hand and much more money. He was to set up a trading colony and convert the natives to Christianity. The fleet consisted of 17 ships (including the *Niña*) and at least 1,200 men. They sailed from Cadiz on September 25, 1493.

Columbus found some gold on his return to Haiti, and he discovered Jamaica and Puerto Rico. He made two more voyages to the New World—in 1498 and 1502. On the third voyage, he discovered Trinidad and set foot on the South American continent. But he never found the Grand Khan or the fabled Indies of his dreams. And he never received the money he had been promised. He died on May 20, 1506, a sad and bitter man.

ATLANTIC OCEAN

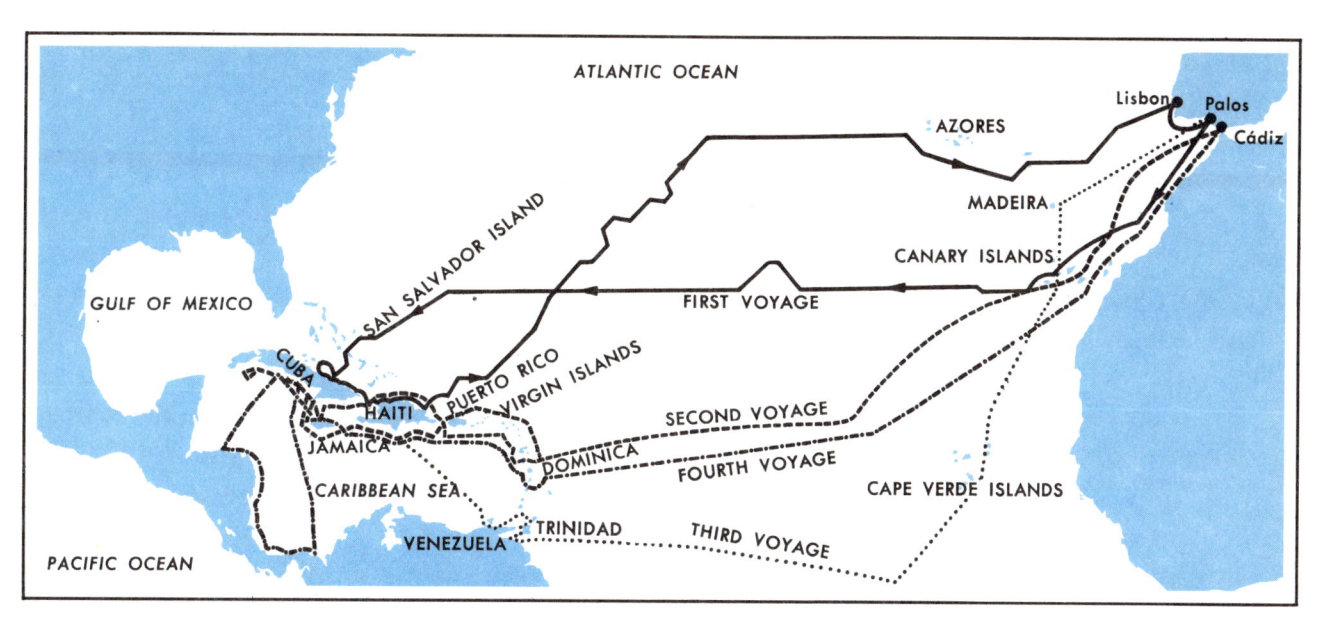

Lisbon
Palos
Cádiz
AZORES
MADEIRA
CANARY ISLANDS
SAN SALVADOR ISLAND
GULF OF MEXICO
FIRST VOYAGE
CUBA
PUERTO RICO
HAITI
VIRGIN ISLANDS
JAMAICA
DOMINICA
SECOND VOYAGE
CARIBBEAN SEA
FOURTH VOYAGE
CAPE VERDE ISLANDS
VENEZUELA
TRINIDAD
THIRD VOYAGE
PACIFIC OCEAN

AMERICI VESPVCII

# THE ROAD TO THE INDIES

I've just told you how Spain tried to find the road to the Indies by sailing west. The Portuguese, on the other hand, hoped to reach the Indies by sailing east, around Africa.

As early as 1482, a Portuguese navigator named Diogo Cam had sailed down the west coast of Africa. But Cam had been unable to sail farther than Walvis Bay in present-day South West Africa (Namibia).

Five years later the trail Cam had blazed was followed by another Portuguese seaman, Bartholomeu Dias, a member of the court.

Dias sailed in August, 1487, in command of a fleet of three ships. Near Walvis Bay, they were caught in a storm and blown far to the south. When the storm was over, Dias tried to return to his original course by sailing east again. But now there was nothing but the open ocean as far as the eye could see. Without realizing it, they had rounded the southernmost tip of Africa. Dias gave orders to sail on.

But one of the ships had been lost in the storm, and the frightened crewmen forced Dias to turn back. On the home-

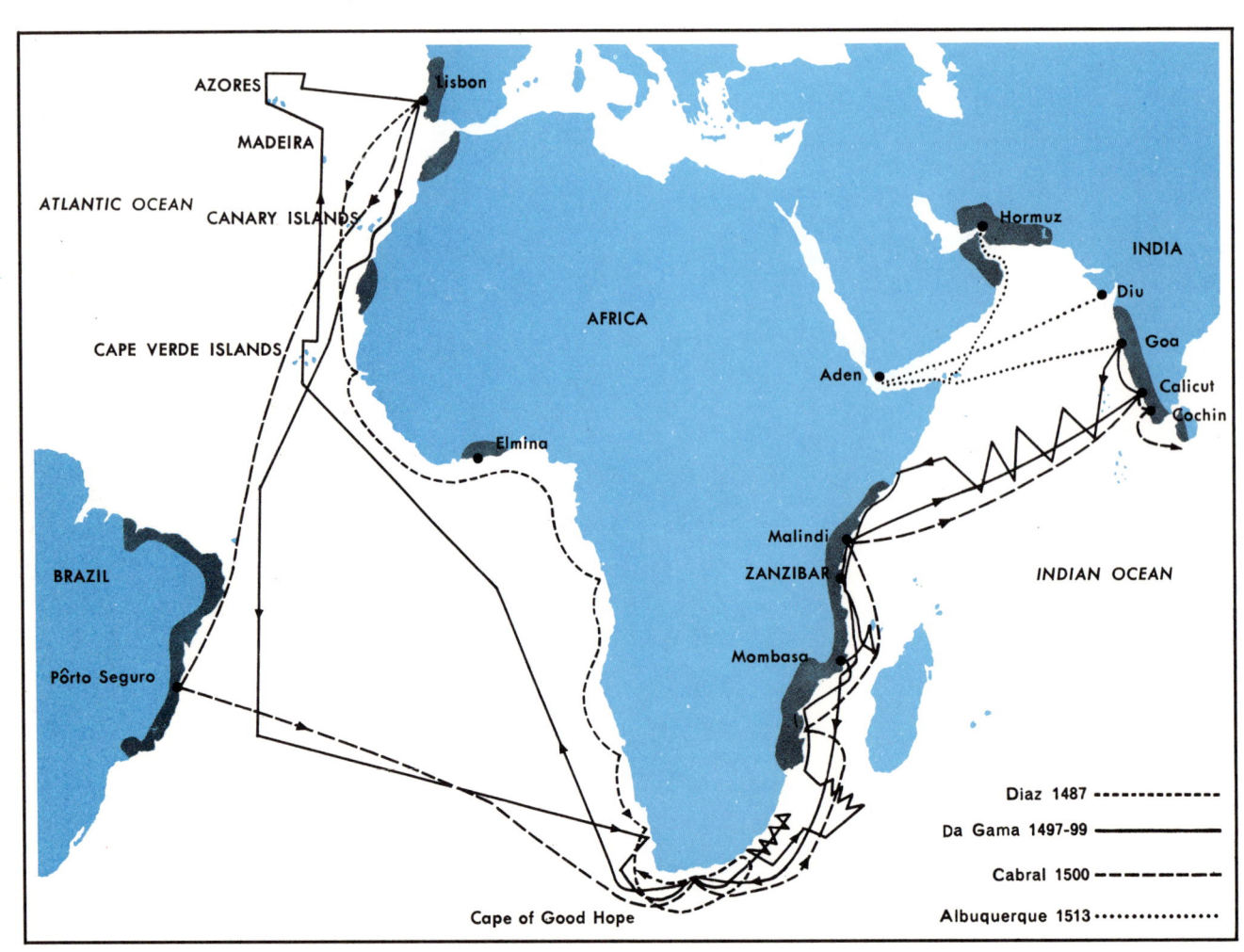

*Opposite page: Vasco da Gama, the Portuguese navigator who opened the sea route to India by sailing around Africa.*
*Above: The routes taken by Bartholomeu Dias, Vasco da Gama, Pedro Alvarez Cabral, and Affonso de Albuquerque. The last two set up trading posts in India. Albuquerque also discovered the Moluccas, or Spice Islands.*

ward trip, Dias named the tip of Africa the Cape of Storms. The Portuguese king renamed it the Cape of Good Hope—for his hope of reaching the Indies by sailing around it.

In 1492 the news of Columbus' first voyage arrived in Portugal. The reports struck Portugal like a flash of lightning. A Spanish fleet under an Italian navigator had taken an untried westward route to the Indies!

The Portuguese weren't going to accept defeat at the hands of their Spanish rivals. A young seaman named Vasco da Gama was given command of four ships and sent to continue Dias's explorations.

The fleet, with some 170 men aboard, left Lisbon on July 8, 1497. After rounding the Cape of Good Hope, they sailed on, up the east coast of Africa.

The fleet stopped at Mozambique and Kenya, and then set out across the vast Indian Ocean. Ten months later, in May, 1498, they reached the port of Calicut on India's southwest coast.

Now, don't get the idea that this voyage was a kind of pleasure cruise! There were terrible storms at sea and two of the ships sank. Also, many of the crewmen died of scurvy, a disease caused by the lack of vitamin C, usually supplied by fresh fruits and vegetables in their diet.

Problems continued on land. The expedition ran into trouble at every port where they stopped. At that time most of the trade on both sides of the Indian Ocean was controlled by the Arabs. At first some of the African and Indian rulers seemed willing to trade with Da Gama. But the Arabs feared that the Europeans would take away their valuable trade in spices. They were also afraid that the Europeans would bring Christianity into the area. They threatened the African and Indian rulers, and trading became very difficult for Da Gama and his men.

But Da Gama did manage to obtain a large load of spices. He sailed for Portugal in August, 1498, and he reached the port of Lisbon about a year later.

Though four ships had set out on the voyage, only one came back. Many crewmen had died. Da Gama had sailed almost 24,000 miles. He had been at sea for more than 300 days, with long periods out of sight of land. He had discovered the sea route to the Indies and had given Portugal control over it.

A year later another fleet was sent out. This one was headed by Pedro Alvarez Cabral, and one of its 13 ships was commanded by Bartholomeu Dias. Near the Cape of Good Hope, violent storms struck again. Four ships went down, including Dias's. The story of Dias's and Da Gama's expeditions was told by the 16th-century poet Luiz Vaz de Camöens. His beautiful *Os Lusiadas* ("The Portuguese") is considered Portugal's national epic.

In 1513 the fabled Spice Islands, or Moluccas, were discovered in the Indian Ocean by an expedition led by Affonso de Albuquerque. A young Portuguese soldier named Ferdinand Magellan went along on that expedition. He later carried out one of the bravest deeds in history.

*Aerial view of the Cape of Good Hope, at Africa's southern tip. The cape was first rounded by Bartholomeu Dias in 1488. Blown off course by a gale, Dias' fleet sailed around the tip of Africa by accident while trying to regain its course. Dias sighted the cape on the return voyage and named it the Cape of Storms. The Portuguese king renamed it Cape of Good Hope. Dias later drowned in a storm off the cape he discovered.*

# THE FIRST VOYAGE AROUND THE WORLD

Christopher Columbus had discovered the New World. Another Italian navigator, Amerigo Vespucci, had explored much of the coastline of South America. He was probably the first to realize that it was not part of Asia at all. Then came the Portuguese soldier I just told you about—Ferdinand Magellan.

Magellan believed that there was a strait, or passage, somewhere near the tip of the South American continent. If that strait could be found, it would be possible to go from the Atlantic to the Pacific—to sail west to the Indies.

In 1513 Magellan asked King Manuel I of Portugal to give him a fleet so that he could search for the passage. But the King refused. Then, as Columbus had done in a similar situation, Magellan turned to Spain for help.

In 1518 the Spanish king, Charles I, agreed to finance the expedition. If Magellan could find the passage, most of the spice trade from the Moluccas would belong to Spain. Also, it would be a serious defeat for Spain's great rival, Portugal.

On September 20, 1519, Magellan's fleet sailed from the port of Sanlúcar de Barrameda on Spain's southwest coast. There were five ships, and the crewmen included Spaniards, Portuguese, and Italians. One of the Italians, Antonio Pigafetta, later wrote a description of the voyage called *The Story of the First Voyage Around the World*. Much of what we know about the expedition comes from this book, which was published soon after their return.

The Spaniards and the Portuguese did not get along well. The fleet took 5 months to reach South America. Then cold weather set in and they had to spend the winter at anchor. Some of the other captains grew restless and complained that Magellan was too harsh a commander. They attempted a mutiny, but Magellan crushed it and executed the leader.

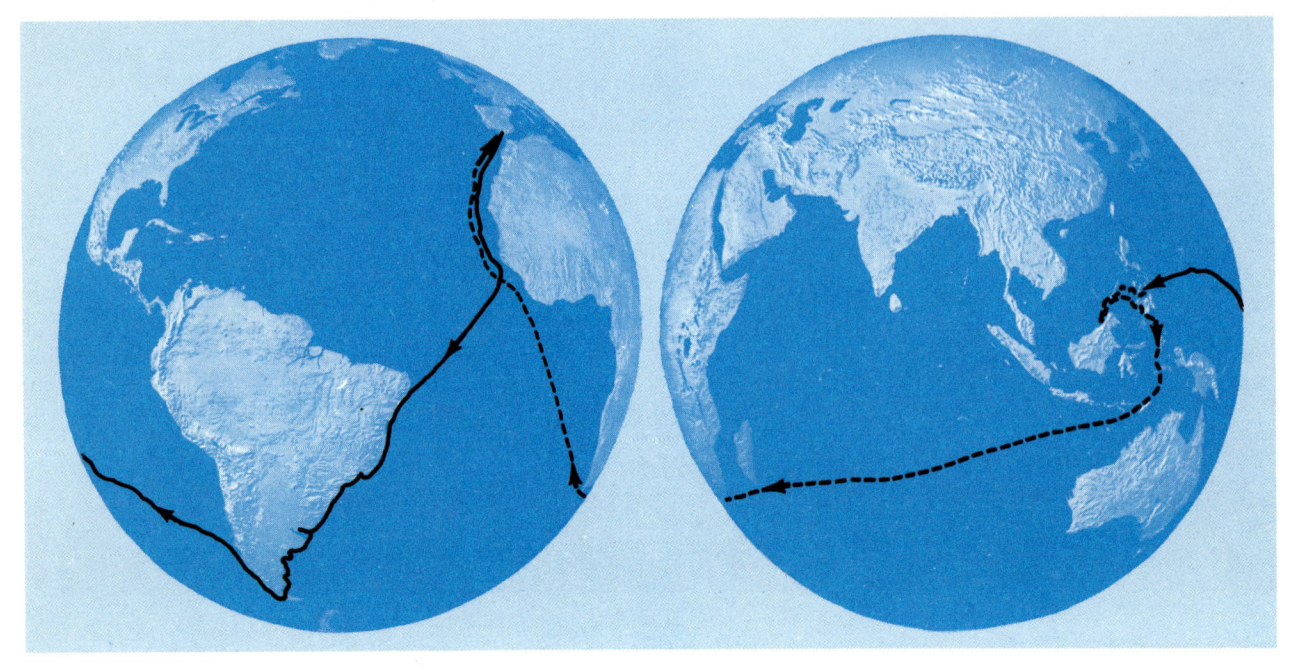

*Above: The route of Ferdinand Magellan's voyage around the world, made between 1519 and 1522. Though Magellan was Portuguese, his voyage was sponsored by Spain. The solid line traces the voyage up to the point when Magellan was killed in the Philippines. The broken line shows the rest of the journey, carried on without Magellan.*
*Opposite page: A portrait of Magellan.*

RD, MAGELLANVS SVPERATIS ANT
FLETI ANGVSTIIS CLARISS.

Only when spring brought warmer weather could the fleet continue its search.

Finally, on October 21, 1520 (the seasons in the Southern Hemisphere are the reverse of those in the Northern), Magellan found a narrow, winding passage. Because of the Indians' fires burning in the distance, Magellan called the area Tierra del Fuego, or "Land of Fire." It took the fleet 38 days to sail through the rocky strait, later named the Straits of Magellan. One ship had sunk earlier and another deserted en route.

The three remaining ships sailed on into an ocean so peaceful that Magellan named it the Pacific. By this time they had almost no supplies left, and many sailors died of scurvy and starvation. At last, on March 6, 1521, they reached the Marianas Islands and took on fresh supplies.

Two weeks later they arrived at the islands we call the Philippines. And there, on April 27, Ferdinand Magellan was killed in a battle between two island tribes. The remaining crewmen chose a Spaniard, Juan Sebastian del Cano, as commander. One ship had to be abandoned and another disappeared. Sailing

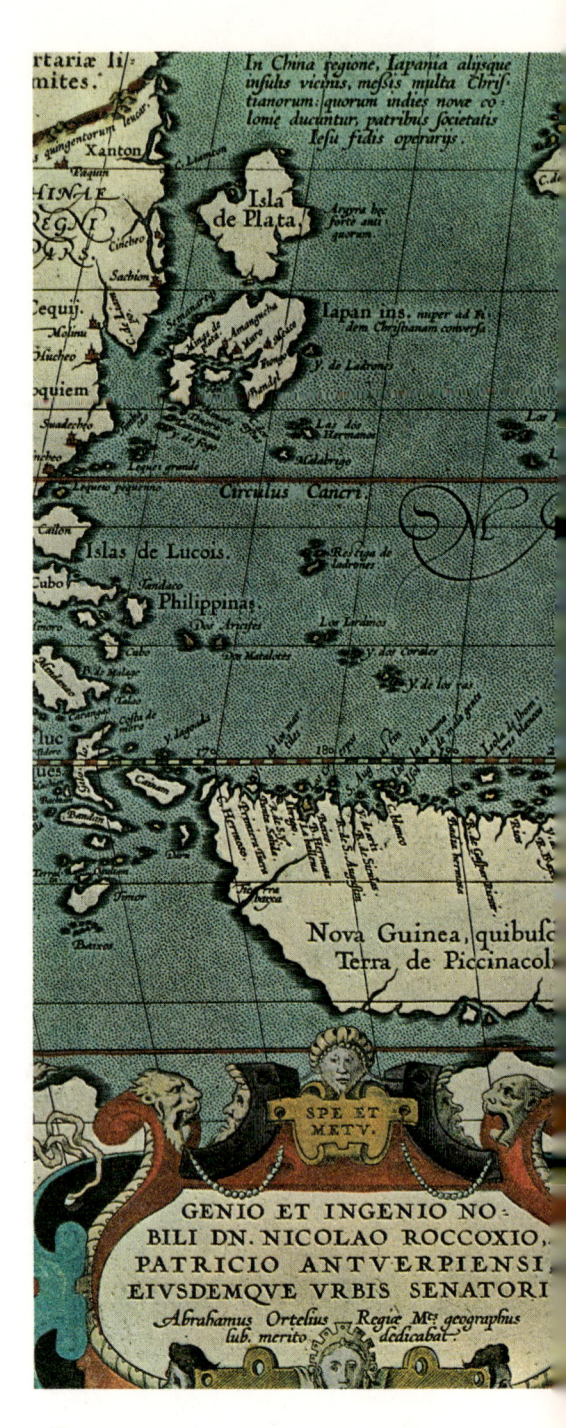

*Above: A 16th-century map of the Pacific Ocean—also known at that time as the South Sea. In mid-ocean is a drawing of Magellan's ship* Victoria, *which successfully completed the first voyage around the earth. This voyage proved once and for all that the world is round. Part of the inscription beneath the ship says, "I have a right to be called Victoria: my sails are wings; my reward is glory; my battlefield is the sea."*

on the *Victoria*, they reached the Moluccas and loaded the ship with spices and food. Cano decided to reach home by sailing west.

On September 6, 1522—almost 3 years after she left—the *Victoria* arrived in Spain. For the first time in history, a ship had sailed around the world. But a high price had been paid. About 250 men had left on the expedition, and only 18 returned. Ferdinand Magellan, who had courageously organized and led most of the voyage, was among the dead.

## THE MAN WHO SEARCHED FOR THE STARS

I want to tell all of you boys and girls about a man whose life was a true success story—he rose from cabin boy to ship's

*Captain James Cook was probably the first of the great explorers who was more interested in the scientific aspects of his voyages than in discovering new lands. Even so, he did discover the Hawaiian Islands and the east coast of Australia.*

In his spare time Cook studied mathematics, astronomy, and geography. Because of his knowledge in these fields, he was selected to head a scientific expedition to the Pacific in 1768. The main purpose of the voyage was to observe the passage of the planet Venus between the earth and the sun, a rare event. But Cook also had special orders from the navy to search for new lands in the southern Pacific between New Zealand and South America.

Cook sailed from England on the H.M.S. *Endeavour* on August 26, 1768. In those days British ships were not very clean and the sailors suffered from disease and vermin. But Cook changed that. He had his crew bathe regularly, and he put the men to work cleaning the ship and killing rats and insects. Cook also took action to prevent scurvy, a serious disease

captain. His name was James Cook and he was one of the greatest explorers of all time. In the 1700's he sailed over large areas of the Pacific and made very accurate maps of that region. He discovered new lands, including the east coast of Australia and the Hawaiian Islands. His voyages laid the groundwork for British colonies in Australia and also in New Zealand.

But we're getting a little ahead of ourselves. So let's turn back the clock to 18th-century England. Our story begins in 1728, the year James Cook was born. The Cook family was poor and James received little schooling. At the age of 12 he went to work as an errand boy in a small shop. Later he got a job with a shipping company. When war broke out between France and Britain in 1755, Cook joined the navy as an ordinary seaman. He received several promotions and became master of his own ship in 1759.

caused by a lack of what we now know as vitamin C. He fed his men raw cabbage and other foods containing this vitamin. Cook won his battle against scurvy. Not a man was lost from this disease during the eight-month voyage around Cape Horn to the Pacific.

Cook arrived in Tahiti in the spring of 1769. He carried out his mission to observe the planets and was nicknamed "he who searches for the stars" by the friendly Tahitians. Next, Cook sailed off to explore the coast of New Zealand. In 1770 he reached the unknown east coast of Australia, which he claimed for England and named New South Wales.

In 1771 Cook returned to England. He was hailed for his feat and promoted to captain. The following year he sailed again, in command of two ships. This time he went in search of a continent that some geographers thought was located in the South Seas near the South Pole. Cook found no such continent but he discovered New Caledonia and Norfolk Island. He also became the first man to sail across the Antarctic Circle.

In 1776 Cook went on his last voyage. He discovered the Hawaiian Islands in January, 1778, and then explored the west coast of North America. At the end of 1778 he returned to the Hawaiian Islands. While there he was killed in a dispute with some islanders. He was buried at sea on February 15, 1779.

*Drawing of Captain Cook's fleet dropping anchor off a coastal village in the Hawaiian Islands, which Cook named the Sandwich Islands. When Cook first visited the islands, in 1778, he found the people to be friendly, though they would sometimes take his possessions. After leaving Hawaii, Cook sailed to the west coast of North America and up through the Bering Straits. A year after his first visit, Cook returned to Hawaii. The inhabitants took one of his canoes, and when Cook tried to get it back, they murdered him. His crew buried him at sea, in accordance with naval tradition.*

# IN DARKEST AFRICA

Now we are going to jump from the waters of the Pacific Ocean to another part of the world. Better put on your warm weather clothes, boys and girls, because we are going into the steaming jungles of Africa. I am going to tell you about David Livingstone, a minister and doctor who went to Africa to help the people and explore the Dark Continent.

David Livingstone was born in Scotland on March 19, 1813. He studied medicine at Glasgow University and received his degree in 1840. He was also ordained a minister that same year and he decided to become a medical missionary. (A missionary is someone who travels to

*Opposite page: David Livingstone, Scottish medical missionary and explorer, who was the first man to cross Africa. He traveled from west to east and explored the Zambezi River basin.*
*Above: Painting by Thomas Baines, showing Livingstone's steam launch, the Ma-Robert, meeting with a wild elephant on the Zambezi. Baines was a member of Livingstone's expedition and made many paintings and drawings of places Livingstone visited.*

*Livingstone's expeditions were full of dangers. The drawing above shows a hippopotamus upsetting his boat. By a miracle Livingstone managed to save himself from the crocodile-filled river.*

other lands to spread religious beliefs.) Livingstone arrived in Africa in 1841. He went to the jungle villages to cure the people of disease and to teach them about Christianity.

Livingstone also became an explorer. He journeyed into what he called "the dark interior" of the African continent, where no other white man had ever set foot. In 1849 he discovered Lake Ngami in the Kalahari Desert of South Africa. Moving north, he discovered and explored the Zambezi River. From 1853 to 1856 he traveled across the breadth of Africa, from Angola to Mozambique. One of his discoveries in that period was the Victoria Falls, which Livingstone named after the Queen of England.

Livingstone visited England in 1857 and found that he had become famous. He was invited to visit the royal family. Scholars asked him to speak at their meetings. In 1858 the British Government put him in charge of an expedition to explore the Zambezi and neighboring rivers. On this expedition Livingstone discovered Lake Nyasa (now Lake Malawi).

In 1864 Livingstone again returned to England. There he learned that another explorer, John Speke, claimed to have found the source of the Nile River—a mystery geographers had long wanted to solve. Livingstone went back to Africa to find out for himself if Speke's claim was true.

## A TIME OF HARDSHIP

Early in 1866 Livingstone began his own search for the source of the Nile. He traveled north from Lake Nyasa to Lake Tanganyika. Along the way he ran into many difficulties, including heavy rains and swarms of tsetse flies. Finally, in 1869, Livingstone became ill and had to be carried on a stretcher to Ujiji, in what is now Tanzania. But after a short rest he went back into the jungle to continue his exploration.

For the next 2 years there was no word from Livingstone. In England and America people asked, "Where is Dr. Livingstone?" James Gordon Bennett, the publisher of the New York *Herald*, decided to find out. He sent Henry M. Stanley, one of his best reporters, to search for Livingstone. Stanley arrived in Africa at the beginning of 1871. He hired about 200 men to carry his supplies and set off across the jungles of East Africa. The journey was full of hardships. But Stanley kept going and 10 months later, on November 10, 1871, he arrived at Ujiji.

## "DR. LIVINGSTONE, I PRESUME?"

Livingstone had returned to Ujiji in October and was there when Stanley arrived. At this point I will let Stanley, in his own words, tell you what happened on that fateful day:

"I pushed my way down a living ave-

Livingstone is found by Henry M. Stanley (center left). Livingstone did not regard himself as "lost," but the outside world had not heard from him for 2 years. When Stanley located Livingstone at Ujiji, he said, "Dr. Livingstone, I presume?"

nue of people" to where "a white man with a long grey beard was standing. As I advanced slowly towards him, I noticed he was pale, looked worried, wore a bluish cap with a faded gold band round it, had on a red-sleeved waistcoat and a pair of grey tweed trousers. I walked deliberately to him, took off my hat, and said, *'Dr. Livingstone, I presume?'* 'Yes,' said he, with a kind smile, lifting his cap slightly. Then we both grasp hands and I say aloud, 'I thank God, Doctor, I have been permitted to see you.' "

Stanley had arrived just in time, because Livingstone had used up his medical supplies. He gladly accepted clothing and other needed items from Stanley, but he would not go back to England while his work in Africa remained unfinished. Stanley later returned to England to write of how he had found Livingstone.

Livingstone remained in Africa to continue his work. He became world-famous for his explorations, during which he covered over 30,000 miles, mainly on foot. He kept a complete record of his travels and made maps of the places he visited. However, he never fulfilled his dream of finding the source of the Nile. In 1872 he set out on another expedition. But his illness grew steadily worse and he died on May 1, 1873.

Livingstone was loved and respected by the African people. When they heard that he was dead, they gathered by the thousands to mourn him and to carry his body to the coast. The funeral procession took 9 months to reach Zanzibar. A British ship was waiting there to carry the body to England. On April 18, 1874, Livingstone's body was laid to rest in London's Westminster Abbey.

*Victoria Falls, on the Zambezi River. These falls, the greatest in Africa, were discovered by Livingstone in 1855. He named them after the Queen of England. The falls had been known before, but Livingstone was the first to make a record of their exact location.*

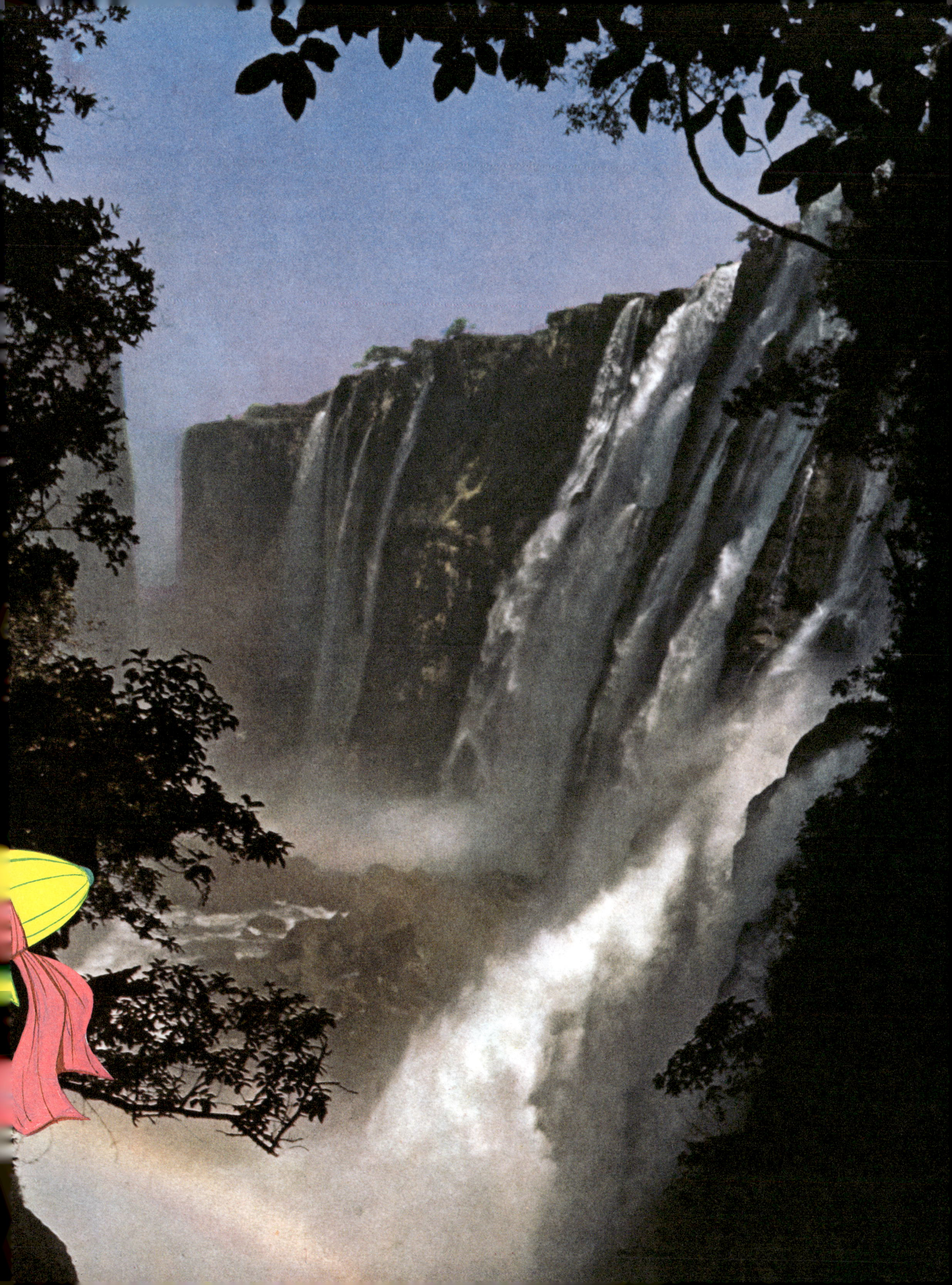

# EXPLORING THE ARCTIC

When I was in school.... Yes, of course I had to go to school! Well, as I was saying, in school I learned that the name Arctic comes from a Greek word meaning "bear." It was chosen because the constellation Ursa Minor, or the Little Bear, shines above the North Pole.

Some of the men who first ventured into this frozen, lonely region were driven by the desire for discovery. Others wanted to win glory for their countries.

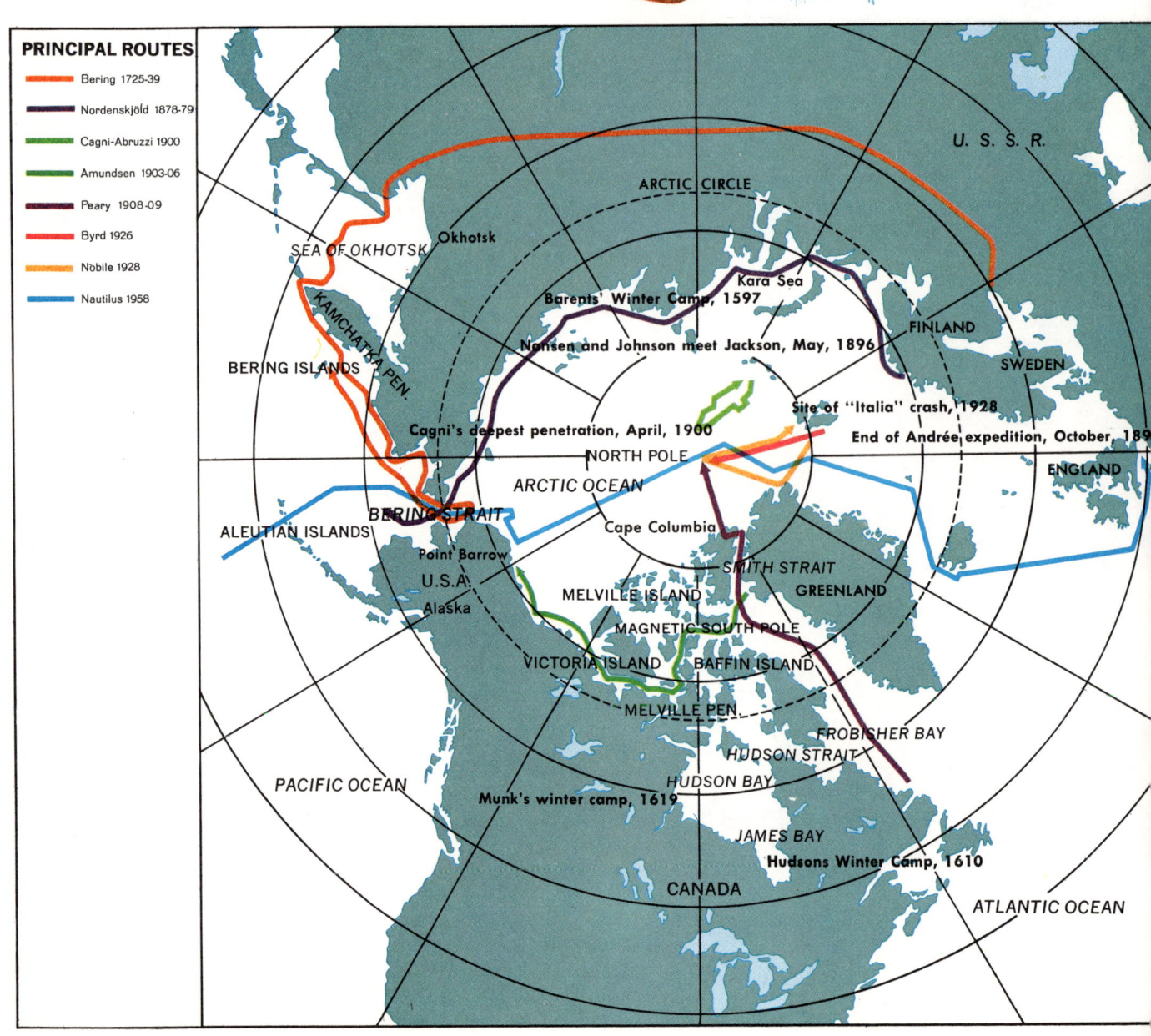

**PRINCIPAL ROUTES**
- Bering 1725-39
- Nordenskjöld 1878-79
- Cagni-Abruzzi 1900
- Amundsen 1903-06
- Peary 1908-09
- Byrd 1926
- Nobile 1928
- Nautilus 1958

82

And still others wanted scientific knowledge. We call these men who sought the northernmost point of the globe Arctic explorers.

## FRIDTJOF NANSEN

Among these brave men was Fridtjof Nansen. His name is considered one of the most important in the history of Arctic exploration. Nansen was born October 10, 1861, in Store-Fröen, Norway, near the capital city of Oslo (then known as Christiania). He later attended the University of Christiania. He studied zoology (animal life) because he loved nature and wanted a profession that would keep him outdoors. He was also interested in sports and spent much of his free time skiing, skating, hunting, and fishing.

After graduation Nansen went on a trip to Greenland. During this voyage he first saw the edge of the Arctic ice cap and decided he had to know what lay beyond it.

After that first voyage, the vast, unknown Arctic was never far from Nan-

*Opposite page: The routes traveled by the major Arctic expeditions.*
*Above: Fridtjof Nansen, Norwegian scientist and Arctic explorer. Between 1893 and 1896, Nansen tried to reach the North Pole. Though he was not successful, he and a companion traveled farther north than any men before them.*
*Above right: The downed balloon of Salomon August Andrée. In July, 1897, he and two other men took off in this balloon from Spitsbergen, hoping to reach the North Pole. Nothing more was heard of them until 1930. Then a Norwegian expedition found their frozen bodies, their log book, and a camera. The film in the camera, developed after 33 years, revealed this photograph.*

sen's thoughts. Just as a compass needle is magnetically attracted to the North, Nansen was attracted by its mystery.

In 1888 Nansen took part in an expedition that crossed Greenland from east to west for the first time. He also learned whatever he could about the Arctic. He decided that the great polar ice cap drifted from southeast to northwest, across the pole. He believed it would be possible to drift along with the ice, straight to the North Pole—like boarding a bus and then getting off when it reaches your stop! Of course, Nansen's plan was terribly dangerous. It involved great risks and took great courage, but I think my example will give you an idea of what he had in mind.

## A DANGEROUS JOURNEY

By 1892 Nansen had worked out his plans for a trip to the North Pole. He presented them to the Norwegian Geographic Society and to England's Royal Geographic Society. Finally the Norwegian Parliament contributed two thirds of the money he needed. The rest was given by the Norwegian people and by King Oscar II.

The ship on which he would make his voyage had to be specially built. Nansen wanted the ship sturdy enough to ride the ice and not be crushed by its pressure, so her hull was made very strong and rounded. He named the ship *Fram*, which is the Norwegian word for "forward."

The expedition sailed from Oslo on June 24, 1893. The *Fram* carried Nansen and a crew of 13, commanded by Captain Otto Sverdrup. They sighted Cape Chelyuskin, the northernmost point of Russia, on September 10. From there they sailed northwest until the *Fram* was caught in the ice near the New Siberian Islands of the Arctic Ocean.

Progress was very slow, and after about a year, Nansen realized he could not reach the pole by ship after all. In March, 1895, he and Lieutenant F. H. Johansen set out with dog sleds and canoes.

The two men pushed forward with

*Opposite page, above: Fridtjof Nansen returns to Oslo after his dramatic polar expedition.*
*Opposite, lower left: A sketch made by Nansen in his notebook showing the stages of his expedition. On April 7, 1895, Nansen and Johansen reached a point very near the North Pole, but bad weather drove them back.*
*Opposite, lower right: Nansen's sketch of "lunar rings" seen during the polar night from his ship, the* Fram, *in November, 1893.*

Vardö
13 August 1896
Fridtjof Nansen

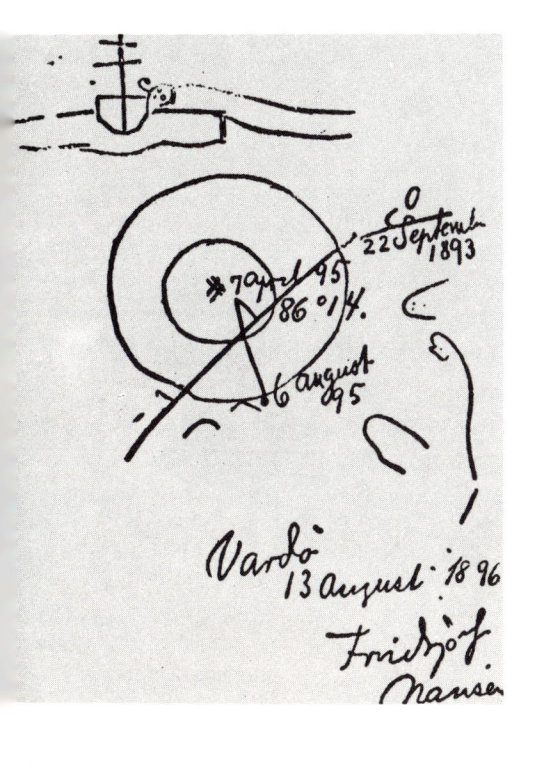

great difficulty. Finally they reached a point that was farther north than man had ever been before. But then, as weather conditions became worse and supplies were growing scarce, they could go no farther. Nansen and Johansen turned west, heading for that part of the Arctic called Franz Josef Land. They built a stone hut and lived on polar bear and walrus meat and fish. It was a hard winter.

In the spring the two men met an English expedition headed by Frederick Jackson. Jackson took them on board his ship, the *Windward*, and they reached Norway safely in August, 1896. The *Fram* was freed from the ice, and Captain Sverdrup sailed her into Oslo a few days later.

Nansen and Johansen's accomplishment thrilled the entire world. They had survived 15 months in the Arctic wilderness. Though they had missed their goal, it had not been through lack of courage.

## RIDING THE WIND

And a young Swede named Salomon August Andrée did not lack courage either. In 1896 he got the daring idea of reaching the North Pole by riding the wind—in a balloon.

He and two other men went to the Spitsbergen (or Svalbard) islands, west of Greenland, where they hoped to start their flight. Their first attempt failed. Finally, on July 11, 1897, the balloonists rose into the sky in their craft, the *Eagle*. They were never heard of again.

In 1930 a Norwegian scientific expedition accidentally found the bodies of the three men. The explorers also found Andrée's log book and camera. The log and the film told a tragic tale of suffering and hardship. After the *Eagle* was forced

Opposite page: Robert Peary, the first man to reach the North Pole, April 6, 1909.
Right: The bell from Fridtjof Nansen's ship Fram. Nansen lent the Fram, which had taken him on part of his polar journey, to Roald Amundsen, another explorer, for a voyage to Antarctica.

down, the three men tried to return to Spitsbergen by land. They died on the return journey.

The balloonists lost their lives in the attempt to reach the Pole. As you will see, the Pole was to claim other victims.

## PEARY CONQUERS THE POLE

At about the same time as the Nansen expedition, a young American naval officer, Robert Edwin Peary, came across a book about Greenland. Soon he, too, was fascinated and attracted by the North. In spite of the dangers and difficulties, sometimes the quest for adventure is almost like a contagious disease.

Peary was born May 6, 1856, in Cresson, Pennsylvania. He worked for the United States Navy as an engineer after graduating from college. But once he was bitten by the "Northern bug," he gave

*Above: Peary and his companions immediately after placing the U.S. flag at the North Pole. Opposite page: Peary's five companions, a black man and four Eskimo, with the U.S. flag and flags of geographical associations.*

up everything but the idea of reaching the Pole.

Peary made his first trip to Greenland in 1886. He later made four more trips, learning all he could about the land and its people, the Eskimo.

The Eskimo knew how to survive in a harsh, unfriendly environment. And they were always willing to help Peary. But the conquest of the Pole was still not easy. Peary made several attempts in the years between 1898 and 1906. Each time he failed. After one expedition, eight of his toes had to be amputated because of frostbite.

Finally, in 1908, Peary was ready to try again. He had learned from his failures, and plans were worked out to the smallest detail. This time he was sure he would make it.

In the summer of 1908, Peary and his party set out for Ellesmere Island, in northern Canada, a spot more than 400 miles from the pole. They sailed on a ship called the *Roosevelt*. When the *Roosevelt* reached the ice shelf, they went on with sleds and dog teams.

Some men were sent ahead as trailblazers. Their task was to build igloos and leave food and supplies at regular intervals. By March, 1909, they had advanced some 300 miles from their base camp. And at the beginning of April, Peary struck out for the Pole. He was accompanied by Matthew Henson, a black man who had been with him on other expeditions, and by four Eskimo.

At long last, on April 6, 1909, Peary planted the United States flag at the North Pole. In his diary, he told of his joy at reaching his goal, writing that he hardly believed the moment he had dreamed of for 20 years had come. Peary felt that it had all been worthwhile.

But they had to return to base camp quickly. The Arctic spring thaw was about to set in, melting the ice, and supplies were getting low. There was little time for rest stops and so little food that they lost a great deal of weight.

Peary returned home in triumph. Honors and praise poured in. He received a national vote of thanks, and the Navy promoted him to the rank of rear admiral.

Peary spent the rest of his life helping other Arctic and Antarctic explorers. He died on February 20, 1920.

## OVER AND UNDER THE POLE

Another famous Arctic and Antarctic explorer was the Norwegian, Roald Amundsen. He had become the first man to reach the South Pole in 1911. After several other expeditions, Amundsen decided to try to reach the North Pole by air. In 1925 his first attempt failed, though he came within 170 miles of his goal.

*The dirigible* Norge, *about to take off on a flight over the North Pole. With Roald Amundsen in command, the party included the* Norge's *designer, Umberto Nobile, and the explorer Lincoln Ellsworth.*

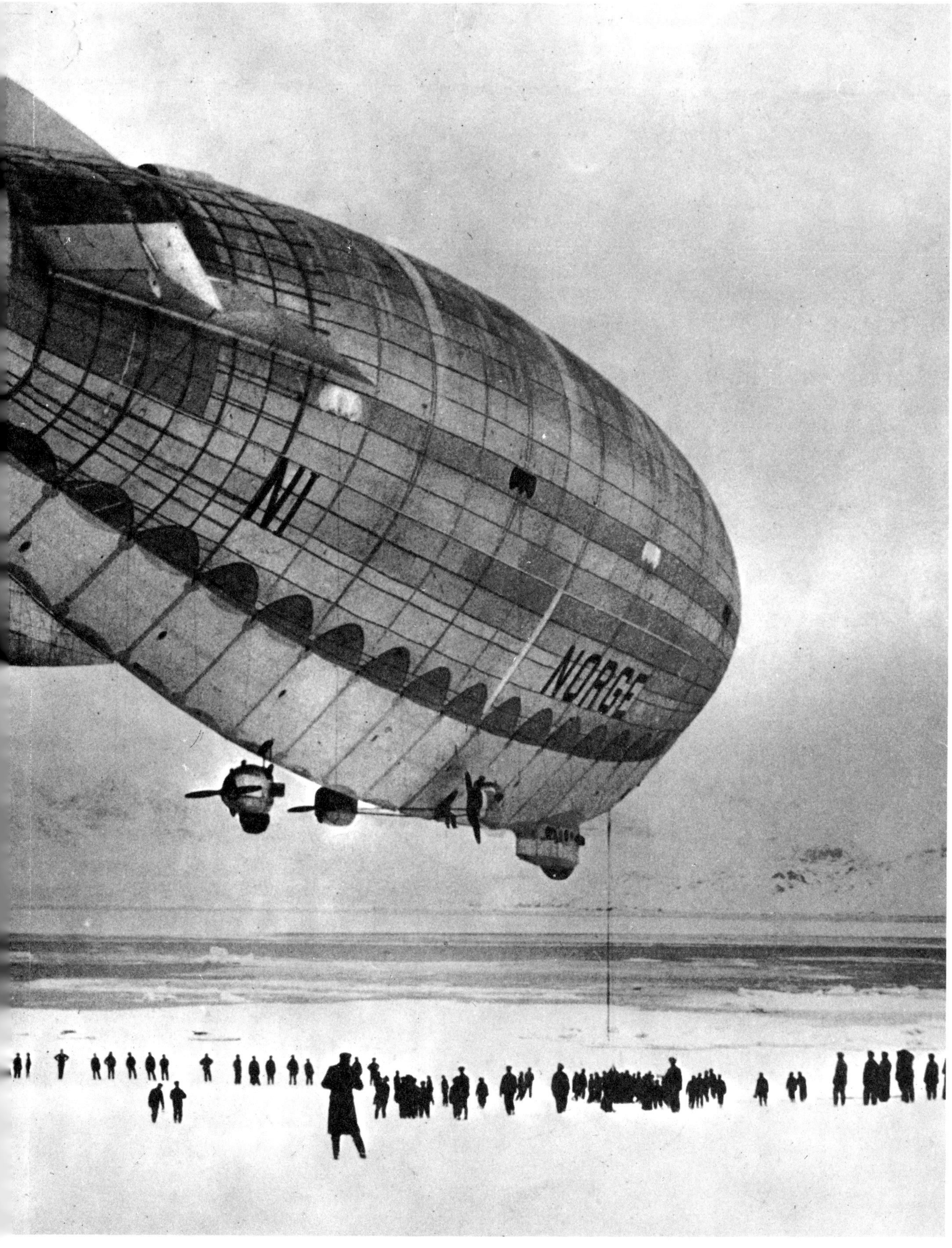
N1
NORGE

*Above:* The nuclear submarine U.S.S. Nautilus, which traveled under the North Pole in 1958.
*Below:* An Arctic sunrise photographed through the periscope of the Nautilus.
*Opposite page:* The Nautilus, *commanded by Captain William R. Anderson, surfaces through the ice against the dark background of the Polar night.*

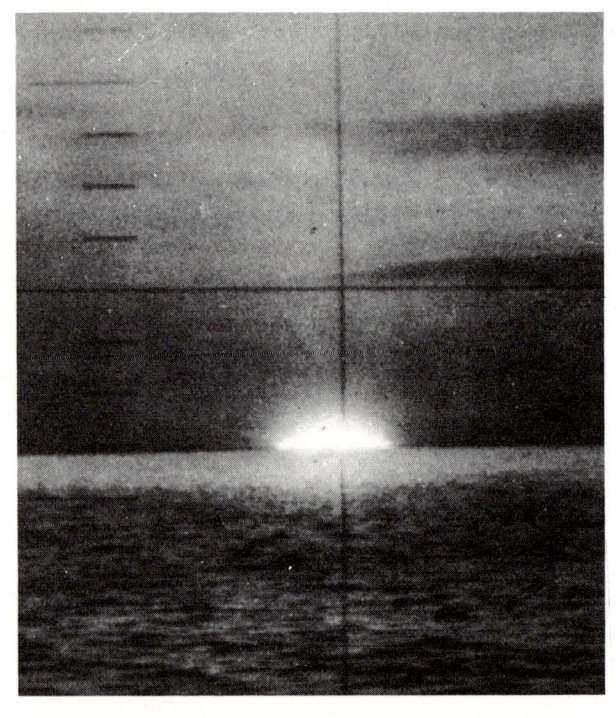

In 1926 he tried again, this time in a dirigible—a large, balloonlike aircraft—called the *Norge*. He was accompanied by the Italian designer of the *Norge*, Umberto Nobile, and an American, Lincoln Ellsworth.

On May 3, 1926, before the *Norge* took off, came the news that an American, Richard E. Byrd, had flown over the pole in a regular airplane. Two days later Amundsen's dirigible accomplished the same feat.

In May, 1928, Nobile tried to fly over the pole in the *Italia*, a new dirigible he had designed. He made three exploratory flights. Returning from the third, the *Italia* lost altitude so suddenly that its cabin was smashed. Nobile and some crewmen were thrown out onto the ice. Then the *Italia* rose again, disappearing forever with those who remained on board.

Nobile and the survivors managed to make radio contact with their base. Relief expeditions were immediately sent by many countries. One of them was led by Roald Amundsen, but his plane was lost and was never seen again. Nobile and his men were finally rescued a month later.

No list of Arctic explorers would be complete without the name William R. Anderson. He was the commander of the U.S.S. *Nautilus*, the first nuclear submarine. On August 3, 1958, the *Nautilus* made history by passing under the North Pole.

## EXPLORING THE ANTARCTIC

Now that we've talked about the North Pole and the Arctic, let's do an about-face and discuss the South Pole and the Antarctic. Of course, that brings us to Antarctic explorers. And here again one of the top places goes to the Norwegian, Roald Amundsen, whom I mentioned before.

In 1910 Amundsen was preparing an expedition to the North Pole. Following

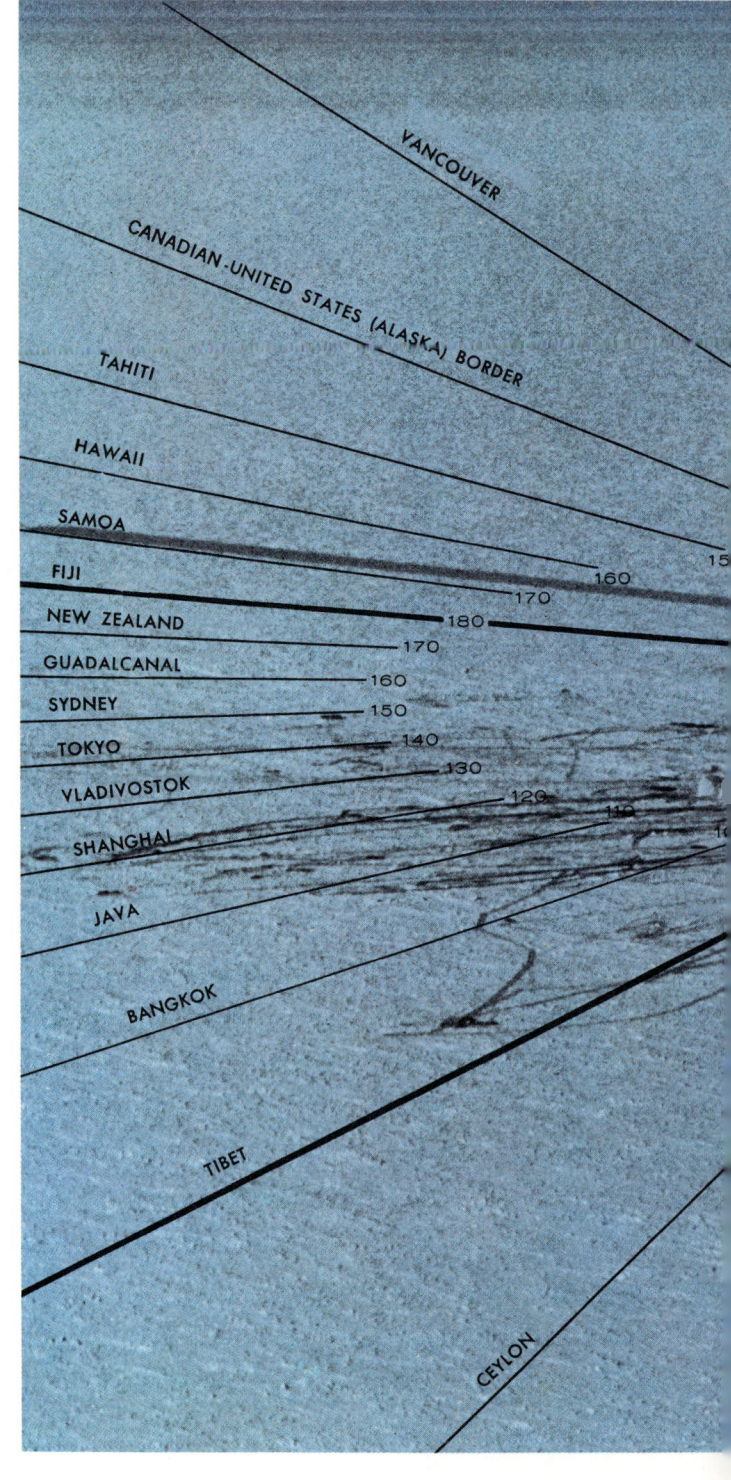

*The South Pole. The lines show the several meridians (imaginary lines running between the North and South poles). The point where the meridians would meet is the South Pole. The Norwegian flag, which Roald Amundsen unfurled on December 14, 1911, is buried there. Amundsen decided to try to conquer the South Pole after Peary beat him to the North Pole.*

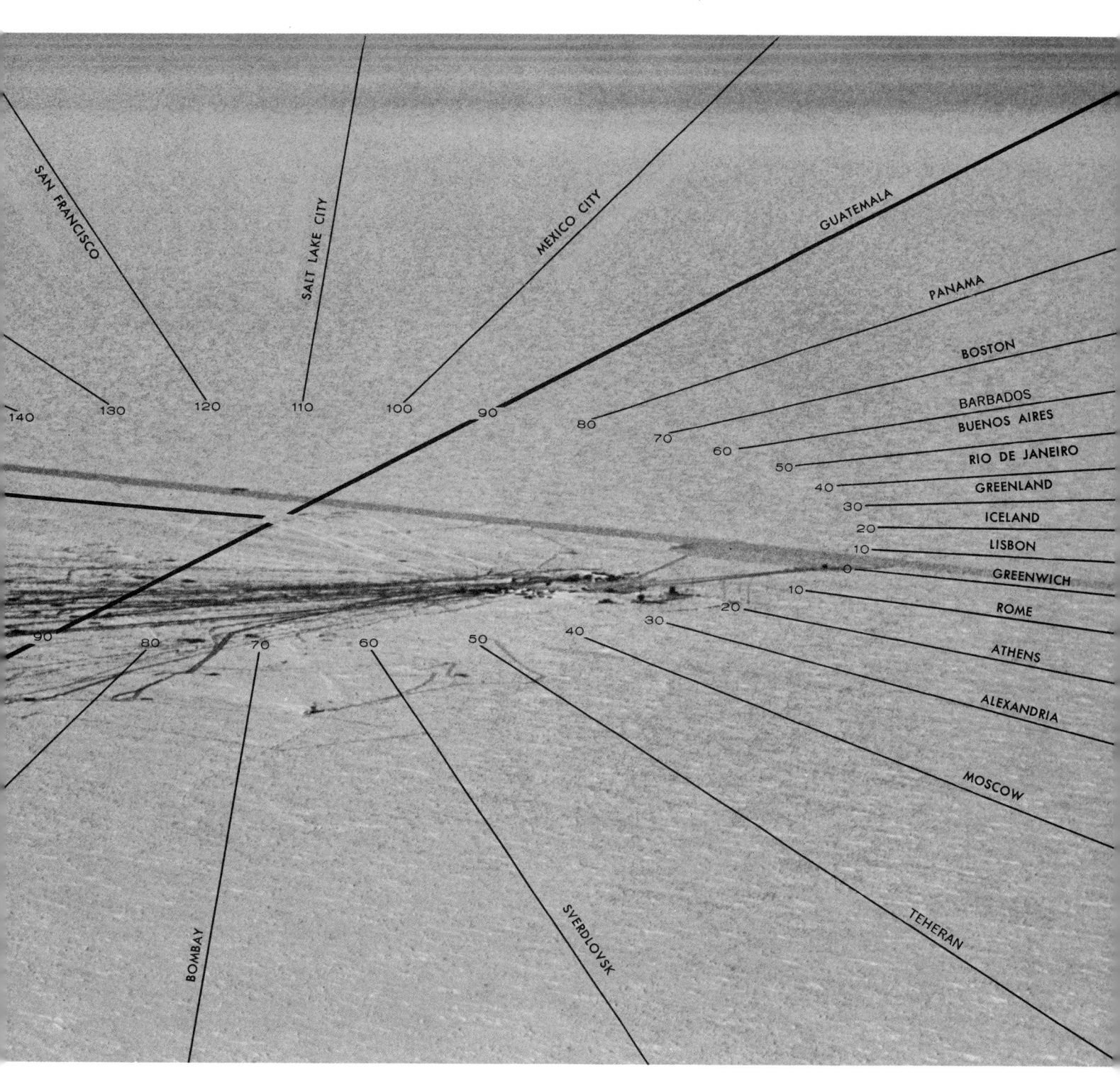

in Nansen's footsteps, and even using Nansen's ship, the *Fram*, Amundsen hoped to be carried to the pole by drift ice. Then the news that Peary had conquered the Pole was flashed around the world. But Amundsen continued his preparations and in June, 1910, the *Fram* sailed out of Oslo.

Not until they were on the high seas did Amundsen reveal his true intentions. Their goal was the Antarctic, and they were going to conquer the South Pole.

When the *Fram* reached the Ross Sea, Amundsen landed near a strip of coastline that was fairly ice free. There he set up a well-supplied base camp and spent several months studying the land. He mapped out the route he would take and made sure there would be food and supplies at regular intervals on the return trip. Amundsen was an excellent organizer. He knew that in order to be successful, nothing must be left to chance.

Finally, in October, 1911, Amundsen and four companions set off across the ice in dog sleds. In November they reached a towering mountain range that seemed to be a major obstacle.

But Amundsen and his men succeeded in finding a way through the mountains. On December 14, 1911, they reached the South Pole.

Their trip back was easy and rapid, thanks to the clearly marked trail and to the food and supply deposits Amundsen had so carefully prepared. I think we might say that his great achievement was due not only to enormous courage but

*Below:* The edge of the huge ice sheet that extends for about 300 miles outward from the South Pole, covering a surface 415,000 square miles in area. It is a continually moving platform of ice. In winter it advances 17 to 19 feet every day and slowly changes appearance. At the end of summer, huge chunks of ice break off from the mass and float away into the ocean.
*Above:* Roald Amundsen and companions prepare to survey the territory before making their final strike for the Pole. They made several such exploratory trips to study the route. They also set up supply bases for the return trip.

also to perfect planning—and perhaps a little bit of luck.

But at just about the same time, luck was not with another famous Antarctic explorer. This unfortunate man was Rober Falcon Scott of England.

## WHITE DEATH

Captain Scott is not the most famous figure in Antarctic exploration, but he is surely the most tragic.

Scott had first gone to the Antarctic in 1901, when he led a British expedition in a ship called *Discovery*. By 1909 he was

*Above left: Roald Amundsen at the age of eight. He was born near Christiania (now Oslo), Norway, on July 16, 1872. His family were seafaring people, and from them he inherited his adventurous spirit. He was stirred by a great ambition to be the first man to reach the North Pole. But when Peary achieved that goal ahead of him, Amundsen changed his objective and set out for the Antarctic. However, he announced his destination to the crew of his ship only when they were well out of port. Above right: An oil painting of Roald Amundsen. Opposite page: Routes of Antarctic expeditions.*

ready for a return trip. He wanted not only to reach the South Pole but also to make a scientific study of the region.

The new expedition was financed by the British Government. Schools throughout Great Britain took up collections to contribute dogs, ponies, sleeping bags, and other equipment. On November 29, 1910, Scott's ship, the *Terra Nova*, set sail from Port Chalmers, New Zealand, en route to the Antarctic.

The *Terra Nova* ran into severe storms soon after leaving New Zealand, and the little ship was tossed and battered by high waves. When they finally reached the Antarctic, they set up their camp at the foot of Mount Erebus, a volcano near the Ross Sea. There they spent the winter making preparations for the trek to the Pole. In November, 1911—about a month after Roald Amundsen left his base camp—Scott and four companions set out for the South Pole.

Scott had gone to the Antarctic mainly for scientific research, though naturally he also hoped to reach the Pole before Amundsen. He and his party moved forward slowly, collecting samples of ice,

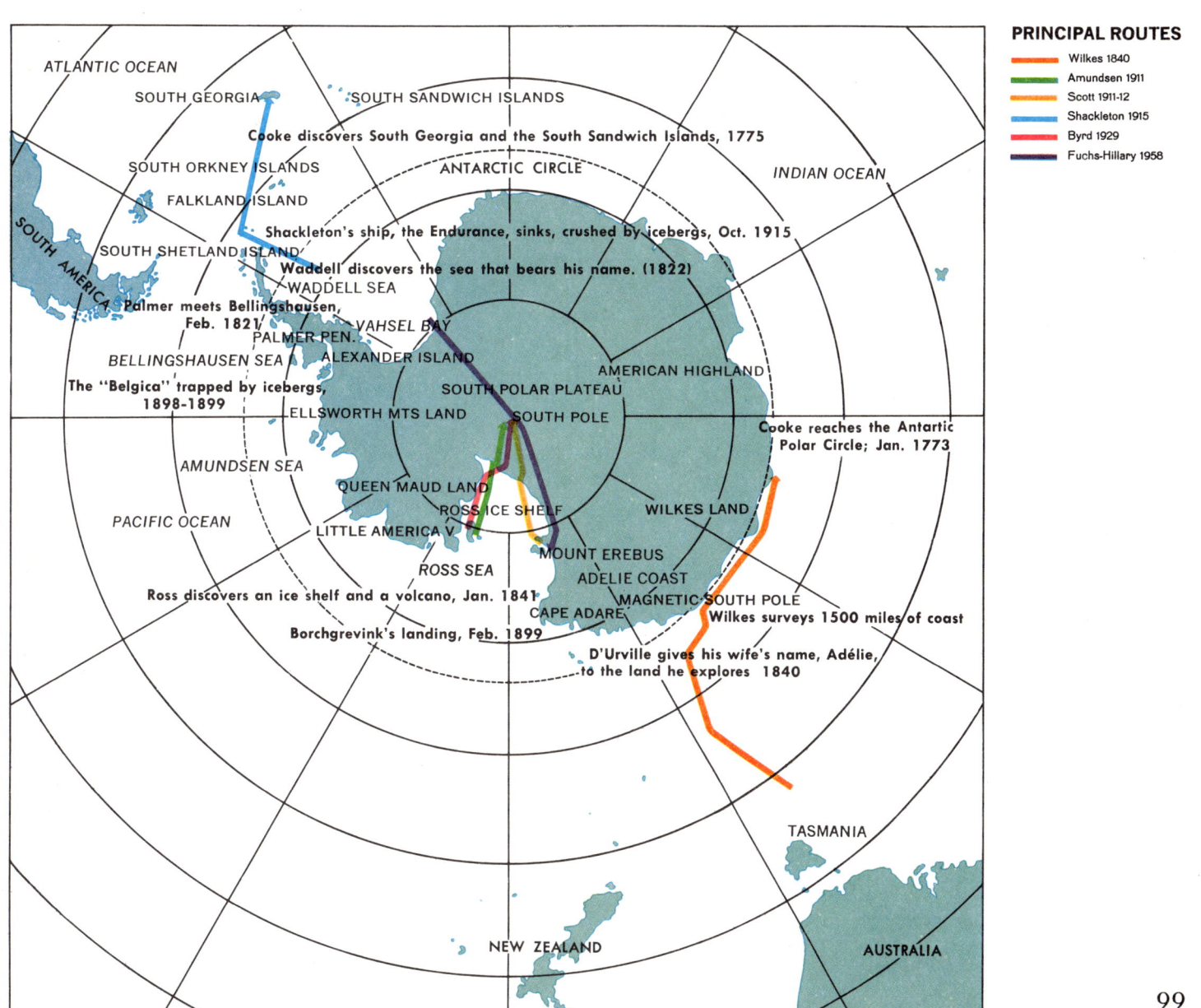

**PRINCIPAL ROUTES**
- Wilkes 1840
- Amundsen 1911
- Scott 1911-12
- Shackleton 1915
- Byrd 1929
- Fuchs-Hillary 1958

99

snow, and frozen subsoil as they went. They also made geographical and meteorological (weather and climate) studies. The weather slowed them down too, for they were met by howling gales and blizzards nearly every day. The effort of pulling the sleds grew more and more tiring.

They struggled on, and finally, on January 18, 1912, they reached the South Pole. But there, waving in the icy wind, was the Norwegian flag! Roald Amundsen had beaten them by a month.

After this great disappointment, the five men started the tragic return to their base camp. It was snowing constantly now and temperatures were far below freezing. Progress was painfully slow.

Crossing the Beardmore Glacier, Edgar Evans, who had seemed to be the strongest of the five, died of exhaustion. At a later rest stop, Captain Lawrence Oates could not go on because of illness. One night he decided not to hinder the others any longer. He quietly left the tent and walked out into the blizzard to his death.

The three survivors—Edward Wilson, Henry Bowers, and Scott—continued their struggle, growing weaker with every passing mile. Finally they could go no farther. They were only 11 miles from a large supply deposit, but another blizzard was raging outside and they were not strong enough to fight it.

One by one, the three men were killed by exhaustion, cold, and hunger. Wilson and Bowers died first. Then Robert Falcon Scott was taken by the white death. It was the end of March, 1912.

Eight months later a relief expedition found their bodies. They also found Scott's journal and the letters he had written to his family and friends and to the families of the other men. The last entry in the journal ends with these words:

"We shall stick it out to the end, but we are getting weaker, of course, and the end cannot be far. It seems a pity but I do not think I can write any more. . . . For God's sake take care of our people!"

*Opposite page: When Robert F. Scott and his party reached the South Pole in January, 1912, they found the Norwegian flag already flying. Amundsen and his party had arrived at the Pole a month earlier.*

*Above: Scott and his party on the final stage of their journey to the Pole.*

*Center: The last page of Robert Scott's notebook. It reads in part, "Had we lived I should have had a tale to tell of the hardihood, endurance & courage of my companions . . . ."*

*Below: Scott and his companions just after discovering Amundsen's camp.*

*Following two pages: A painting representing one of the several expeditions sent to the Arctic between 1848 and 1859 to search for the missing explorer John Franklin.*

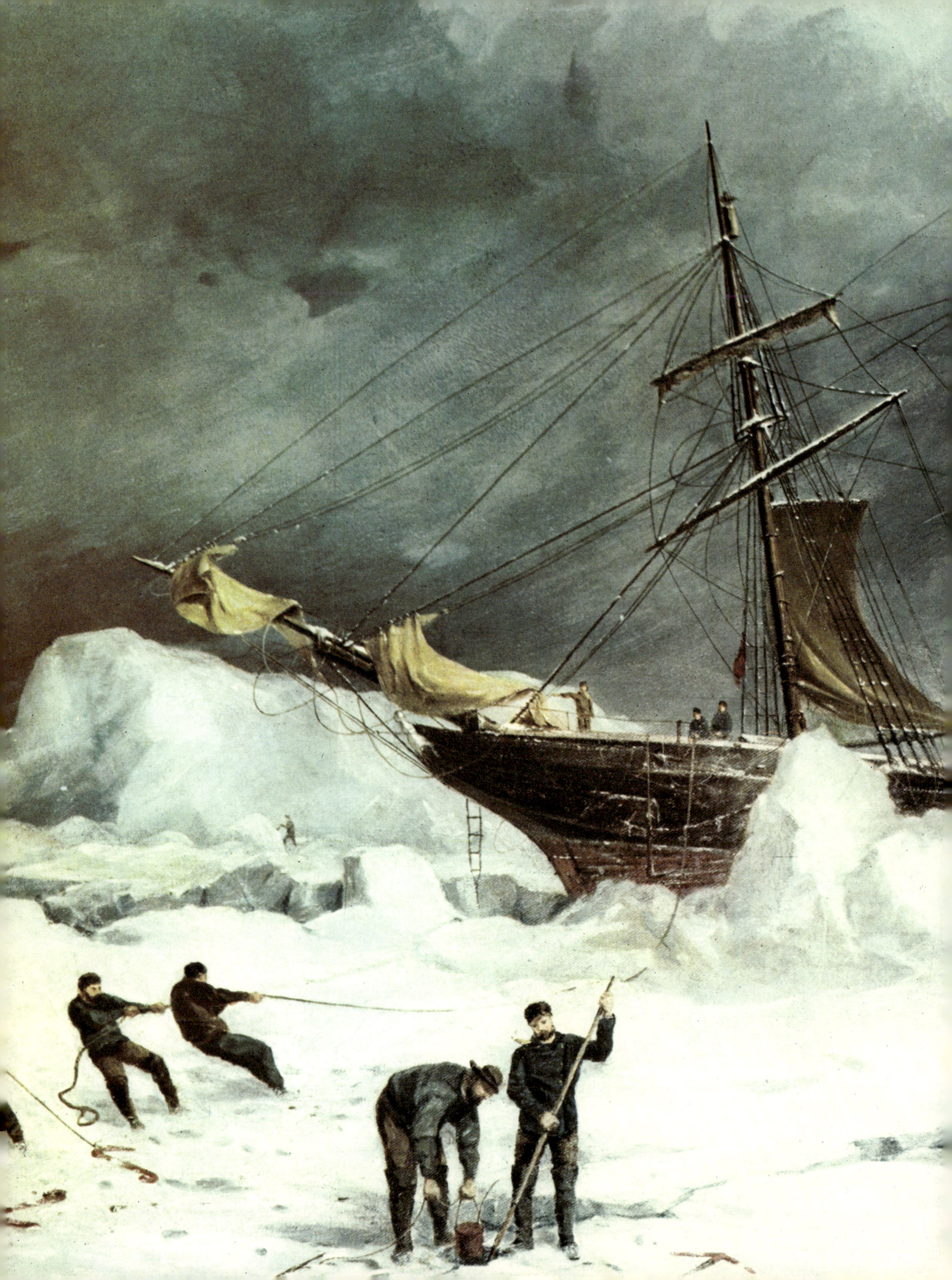

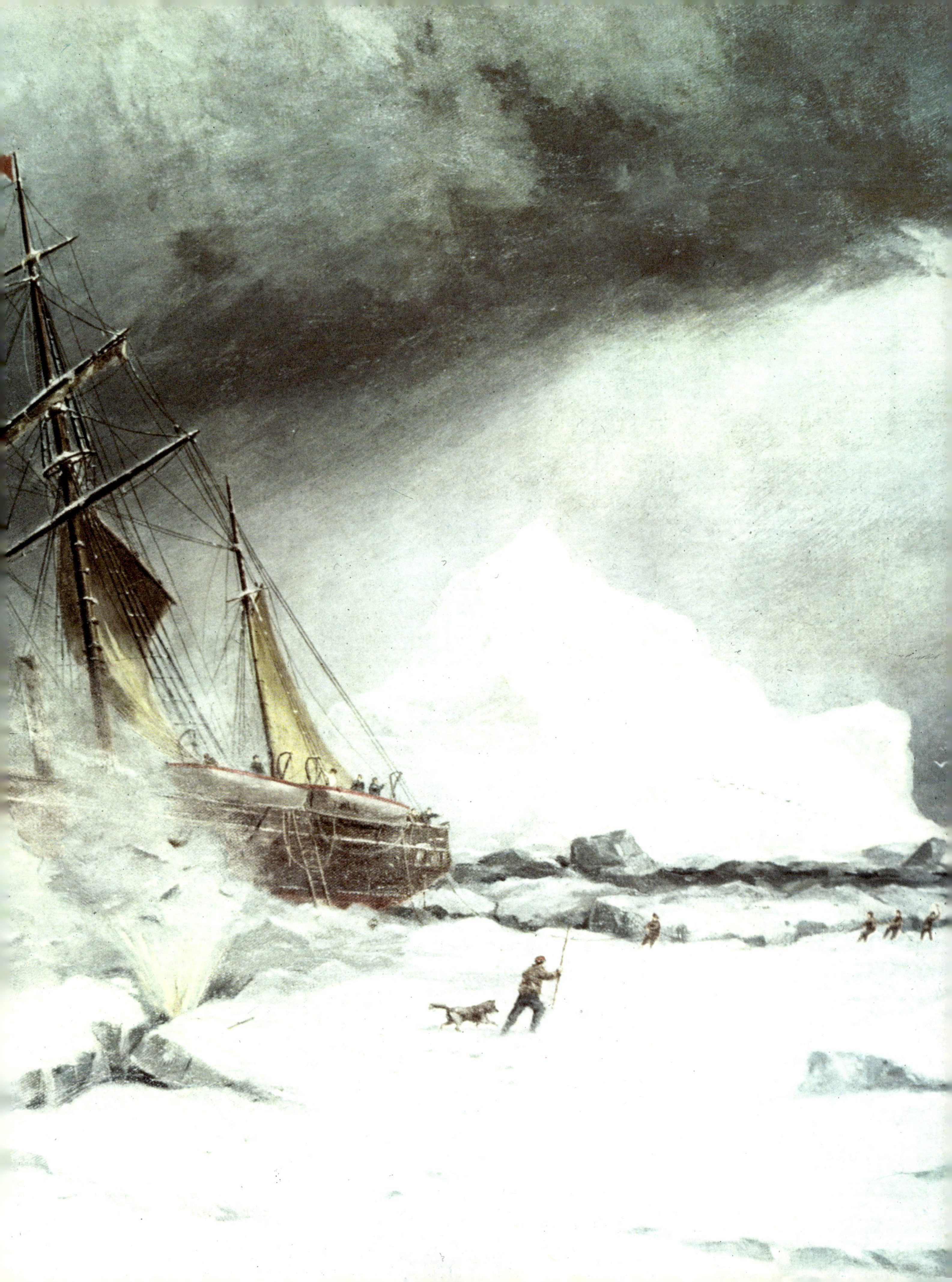

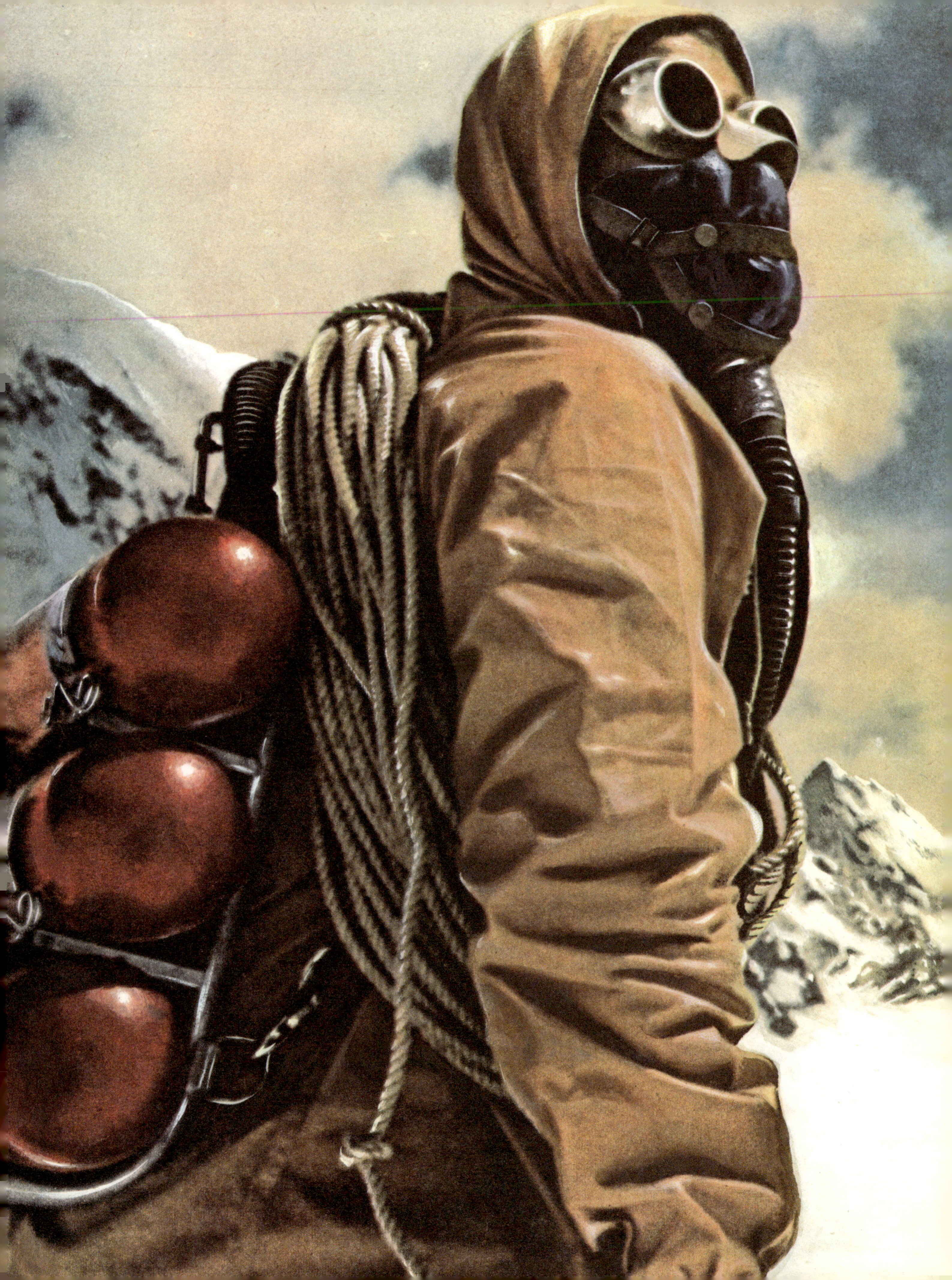

# SCALING THE ROOF OF THE WORLD

In southern Asia, south of the Tibetan highlands and high above the valleys of the Indus, Brahmaputra, and Ganges rivers, soars a great mountain chain. It extends more than 1,500 miles.

Geographers call this mountain chain the Himalayas, but I prefer to think of it as the land of the giants, because it has the highest mountains in the world. At least 40 of its peaks tower 25,000 feet or more. Dominating this army of giants is Mount Everest, on the border between Tibet and Nepal. At 29,028 feet it is the highest spot on earth. The ancient Greeks believed that Mount Olympus, the highest mountain in Greece, was the home of the immortal gods.

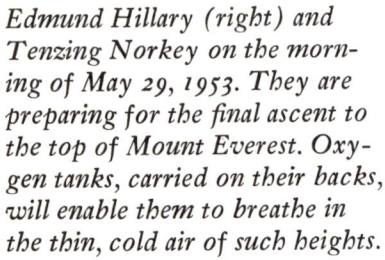

*Edmund Hillary (right) and Tenzing Norkey on the morning of May 29, 1953. They are preparing for the final ascent to the top of Mount Everest. Oxygen tanks, carried on their backs, will enable them to breathe in the thin, cold air of such heights.*

The mountaineers of Tibet believe that Chomolungma (their name for Mount Everest) is the home of the mysterious *yeti*, the abominable snowman.

For many years the challenge of Everest drew the interest of explorers and mountain climbers. But added to the immense physical difficulties of scaling the world's highest peak was the fact that for centuries much of the Himalayas and its surrounding area had been forbidden to foreigners. It was not until 1920 that a British expedition was permitted to enter Tibet to search for a route to Everest.

Between 1922 and 1952 there were a number of attempts to climb Everest. All failed, although a height within 1,000 feet of the summit was reached. Finally, in 1953, a successful climb to the top of Everest was carried out.

It was a British expedition commanded by Colonel John Hunt. One of the members was a New Zealander named Edmund Hillary. The porters and guides were the sturdy Sherpas, a mountain people from Nepal. Outstanding among the Sherpas for his ability was Tenzing Norkey, who had taken part in previous expeditions. He was *shidar*, or chief, of the guides and porters.

Yard after yard the expedition slowly and laboriously struggled upward. Every 1,000 or 2,000 feet, base camps were established. Finally on May 28, 1953, the last camp was set up at 27,900 feet. The next day two men, Hillary and Tenzing,

*A view of Everest, the world's highest mountain, and its surrounding peaks. When Edmund Hillary and Tenzing Norkey finally reached the top of Everest, they were cold and exhausted, but triumphant. They shook hands, embraced, and then slapped each other on the back until they were breathless.*

attacked the final stage of the ascent. At last they set foot on the summit. Everest had been conquered!

But, in the far northeastern end of the Himalayas, in the Karakoram range, the second-highest mountain in the world, Mount Godwin Austen, or K2, still remained unconquered. Its height, 28,250 feet.

In 1954 an Italian expedition under the geologist Ardito Desio attempted what many other mountain climbers had tried and failed—to climb K2.

The expedition's leaders also included Achille Compagnoni and Lino Lacedelli. They endured many dangers and hardships, including the death of one of their companions. But, in the summer of 1954, Compagnoni and Lacedelli planted the Italian flag on the summit of K2.

## FROM THE HEAVENS TO THE DEPTHS OF THE SEA

Thus our planet gradually reveals its secrets to those fearless and determined men who succeed in overcoming hardship and danger in their desire to explore the far corners of the earth.

We should therefore not be surprised if, sooner or later, man attempted to explore the dark and unknown depths of the sea.

One of the first notable deep-sea explorations was carried out by an American, William Beebe. In 1934 he descended over 3,000 feet below the Atlantic Ocean near Bermuda in a bathysphere. The bathysphere was a large hollow cast-iron ball. It was supplied with oxygen, connected to a ship on the

*Left: Tenzing Norkey, photographed by Edmund Hillary on the summit of Everest. Attached to Tenzing's ice ax are flags of the United Nations, Great Britain, Nepal, and India.*
*Opposite page:* The Trieste, *the bathyscaphe used for record ocean descent of 35,800 feet in 1960.*

surface by steel cables, and equipped with observation windows. A dive, in 1949, in the bathysphere reached a depth of 4,000 feet. This record stood for many years, until a Swiss scientist, Auguste Piccard, entered the field of underwater exploration.

Piccard's career spanned two extremes: he explored both the upper reaches of the atmosphere and the lowest depths of the oceans. Before Beebe made his record dive in his bathysphere, Piccard had already won worldwide attention for his daring balloon flights into the stratosphere, the upper layer of the atmosphere that encircles our globe. In his first attempt, in 1931, he reached an altitude of over 10 miles. After numerous other flights, Piccard, beginning in 1937, devoted himself to the study of vehicles that could be used for underwater exploration.

Piccard's work was interrupted by the outbreak of World War II, but he resumed it again after the war ended in 1945. The underwater ship he designed and built was called a bathyscaphe. Unlike Beebe's bathysphere, the bathyscaphe was not connected to a surface ship by cables. Thus it was able to move about underwater. It somewhat resembled a submarine in appearance, but it could dive deeper than any submarine.

To achieve buoyancy (the ability to float or to rise to the surface of the water), Piccard used tanks filled with gasoline, which is lighter than water. To make the ship descend, a form of metal ballast, held in place by magnets was used to increase its weight. When Piccard wanted his bathyscaphe to rise to the surface, the metal ballast was released.

Piccard's first diving attempt failed. But in 1953, together with his son Jacques, he descended over 10,000 feet beneath the surface of the Adriatic Sea in the bathyscaphe *Trieste*.

Later Piccard dove to even greater depths. But his record was finally broken in 1960 by his own son. Jacques Piccard was accompanied in the *Trieste* by an American naval lieutenant, Don Walsh. They descended to the incredible depth of 35,800 feet in the Marianas Trench near the island of Guam, one of the deepest spots in the Pacific Ocean.

After all this, was there still something left for man to attempt?

You bet there was!

# THE ADVENTURES OF THE *KON-TIKI* AND THE *RA*

I must stop for a moment before continuing my story about the exploits that led to the conquest of the skies. I want to tell you about a series of adventures that were both daring and unusual. They resulted from one man's belief in his ideas and his attempt to prove them.

The adventures were inspired by a Norwegian, Thor Heyerdahl. They were unusual because, in the 20th century, he used methods that were centuries old. But he did this on purpose.

In 1947 Heyerdahl crossed the Pacific Ocean from Peru to the islands of Polynesia in a balsa wood raft—a distance of about 6,000 miles.

He called the raft *Kon-Tiki*, after a god of the ancient Incas of Peru. Heyerdahl was trying to prove that the Incas could have made the same journey many centuries ago on the same kind of raft.

Later Heyerdahl attempted a similar journey on a boat made of papyrus, a plant found in the Nile Valley. The boat was named *Ra*, after the chief god of the ancient Egyptians. This time Heyerdahl wanted to prove the existence of a sea route from North Africa to America. He believed that the Egyptians once might have followed such a route, in boats made of papyrus, long before Columbus.

Heyerdahl failed in his first attempt, but he built a second papyrus vessel, the *Ra II*. In 1970 he sailed from the port of Safi in Morocco, with seven companions. After a hazardous journey of some 2 months, they reached the island of Barbados in the West Indies.

*Opposite page: The* Kon-Tiki, *the balsa wood raft on which the Norwegian Thor Heyerdahl crossed the Pacific Ocean, from Peru to Polynesia, in 1947. Right: The* Ra II, *under construction in a Moroccan shipyard. In 1970 Heyerdahl sailed this papyrus boat across the Atlantic, from Morocco to Barbados. He wanted to show that the ancient Egyptians might have used a similar vessel and route, and reached the New World before Christopher Columbus.*

*Above:* Teetering over the edge of the boat, crew member Santiago Genoves tries to adjust the enormous sail of the Ra II.
*Opposite page:* The Ra II, damaged during the difficult voyage, is still hardy enough to brave the giant waves and turbulent waters of the Atlantic.

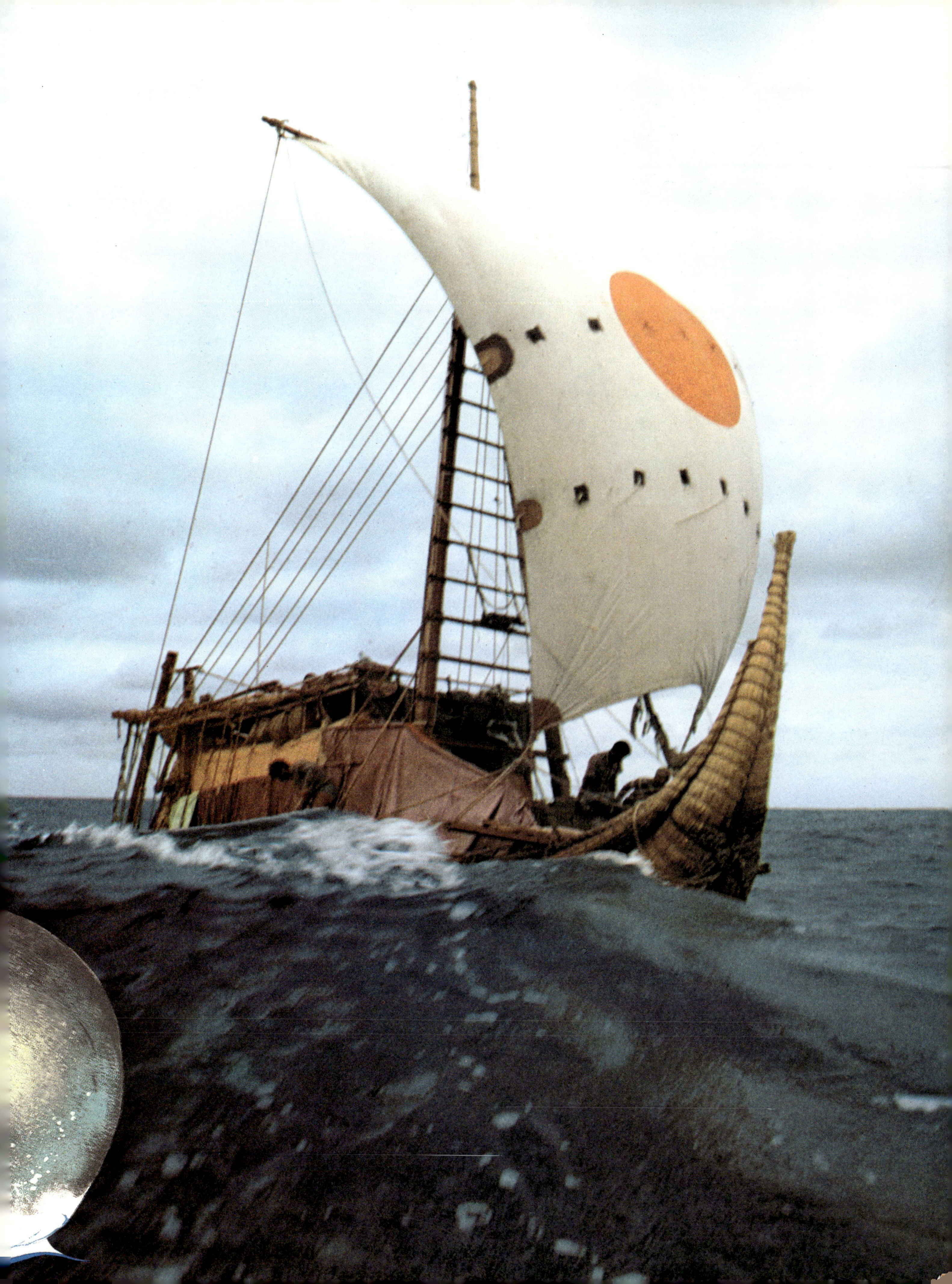

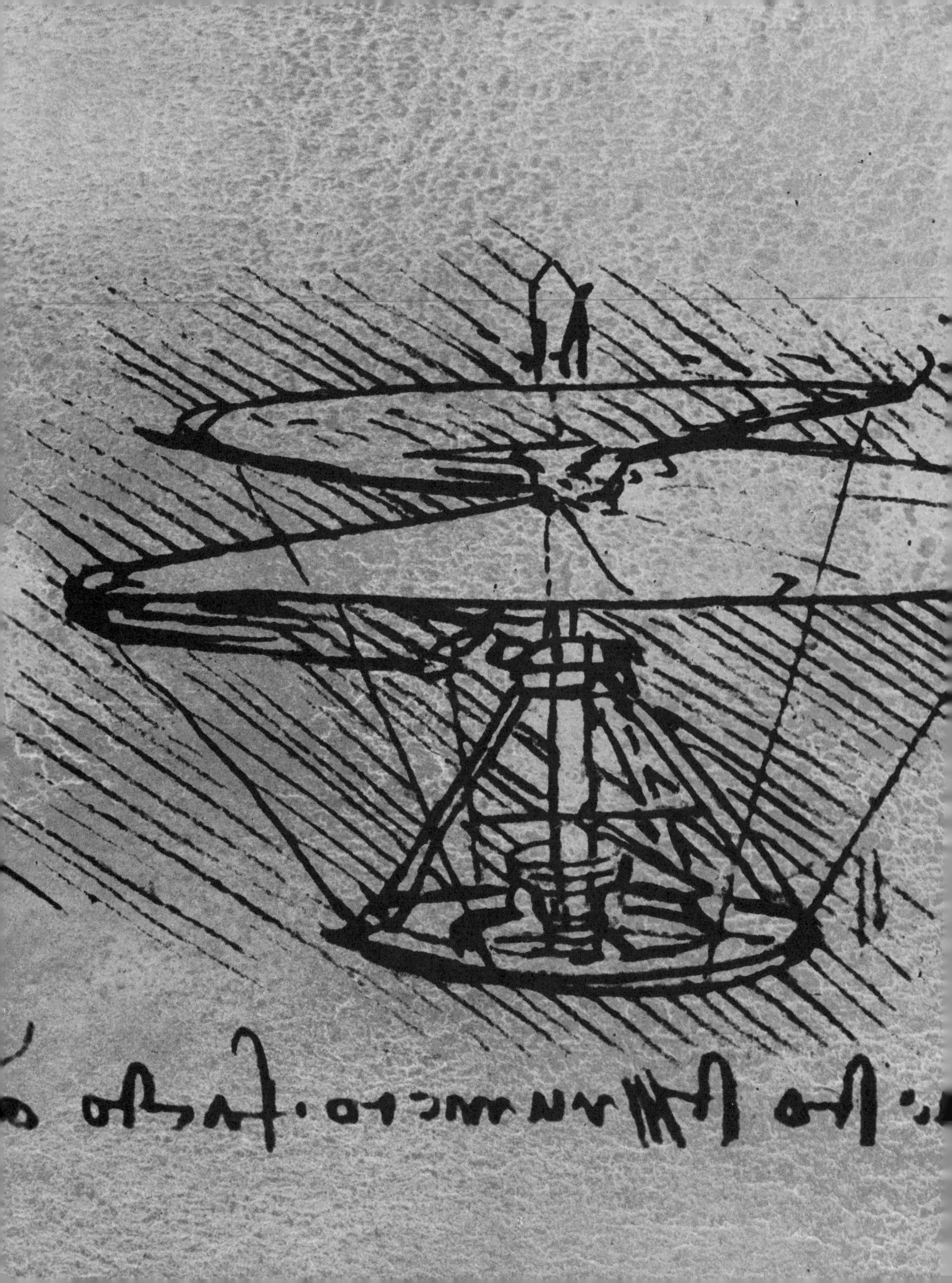

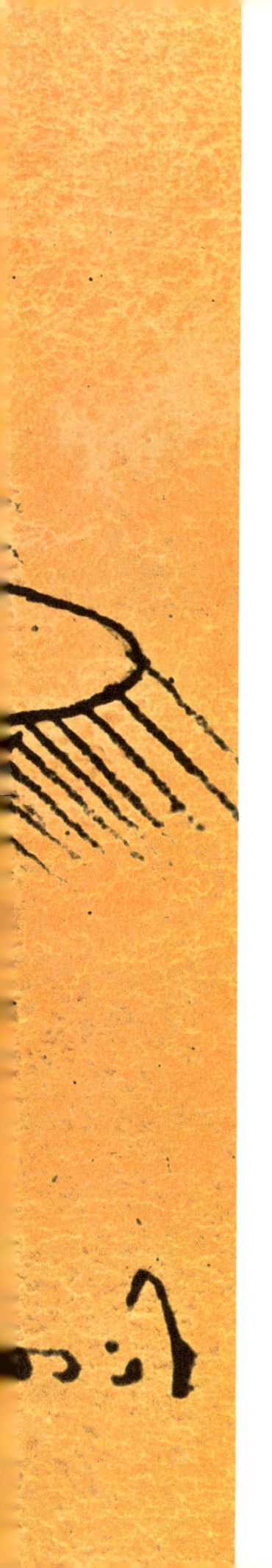

# A PATHWAY THROUGH THE SKIES

I just realized that we're at the last chapter of this book, and we haven't yet gotten around to one of man's greatest adventures—the conquest of the skies.

The idea of human flight is not new. Early man probably looked up at the soaring birds and wondered how they flew—and why he could not. Myths and legends abound with man's attempts to imitate the birds. One of the best-known myths is that of Daedalus and Icarus.

Daedalus was the brilliant Greek artist and engineer who built the labyrinth, a complicated series of passageways, for King Minos of Crete. The King was so pleased with Daedalus' work, however, that he refused to let him leave Crete. So Daedalus built two sets of wings, made

115

of feathers stuck together with glue or wax, for himself and his son, Icarus. With these wings he hoped to escape from Crete. The wings worked well until Icarus flew too close to the sun. The wax holding the wings together melted, and he fell into the sea and drowned. Daedalus reached Greece safely but, grief-stricken at the death of his son, determined never to tempt the gods again by flying.

The myth of Daedalus and Icarus was for centuries a symbol of man's being chained to the earth. Still some men continued to explore the mysteries of flight. The great Italian genius Leonardo da Vinci, about the end of the 15th century, developed scientific theories of flight and designed an early form of helicopter. In the 18th century, two Frenchmen, the Montgolfier brothers, Joseph

*Left: The Wright brothers, Wilbur (above) and Orville (below). Opposite page: A group of dignitaries in front of Sir Hiram S. Maxim's flying machine in 1894. His steam-powered plane later crashed while being tested.*

and Jacques-Etienne, built a balloon that ascended to a height of over 80 feet. It was man's first entry into the realm of the birds.

Then, toward the end of the 19th century, a German, Otto Lilienthal, conducted a series of experiments with gliders. He made some 2,000 glider flights, earning fame as one of the pioneers of modern aviation.

But before a glider could become an airplane, the driving force of an engine was required. Then man could fly as master of the skies, independent of the winds.

## MAN FLIES!

The experiments of Lilienthal and others influenced two Americans, Orville and Wilbur Wright. The two brothers had a printing shop and a bicycle repair shop in Dayton, Ohio. In their spare time they experimented with gliders. After several successful glider flights, they built a machine of wood, canvas, and wire, powered by a 12-horsepower gasoline engine. Building the engine was the most difficult part, for it had to be light. The total weight of the Wright brothers' machine, aptly called *Flyer*, was 750 pounds, including the weight of the pilot. It was lighter and less powerful than a modern automobile.

The brothers tossed a coin to see which one would attempt the first flight. Orville won. On the morning of December 17, 1903, lying face down at the controls, he made the first sustained, powered flight in a heavier-than-air craft. He flew only

120 feet and remained aloft only 12 seconds, but it was a milestone in the world's history. Three more flights were made that day before the *Flyer* was damaged by a gust of wind.

Aviation developed rapidly after the Wright brothers' historic flight. Airplanes grew more powerful; they flew faster and for longer distances.

By the 1920's the feat that drew the world's attention was a nonstop flight across the Atlantic Ocean by a lone pilot. Two Englishmen, Alcock and Brown, had flown the Atlantic in 1919. But it was not until 1927 that one man made the nonstop flight. He was a young American named Charles Lindbergh.

## THE LONE EAGLE

I have just taken a look at a picture of Lindbergh's plane, the *Spirit of St. Louis*. I find it difficult to believe that a man would have the courage to make a flight of over 3,600 miles, from New York to Paris, in such a frail-looking craft. The single engine generated only 220 horsepower. The wings were of canvas stretched over a wooden frame. There were no landing lights, radio, or glass in the cockpit windows. All equipment was kept at a minimum to reduce weight, so that extra supplies of gasoline could be taken aboard for the long flight. Lindbergh's food supply consisted of a few sandwiches and several quarts of drinking water.

For 24 hours before his departure Lindbergh had not slept. He spent the time in last minute preparations. At the moment the gasoline tanks were being filled it began to rain. Lindbergh was ad-

*Opposite page: The* Spirit of St. Louis, *flown by Charles Lindbergh in the world's first solo nonstop transatlantic flight in 1927.*
*Right, above: A 1927 painting of Charles A. Lindbergh.*
*Right, below: Lindbergh is showered with confetti, as he receives a hero's welcome in New York City.*

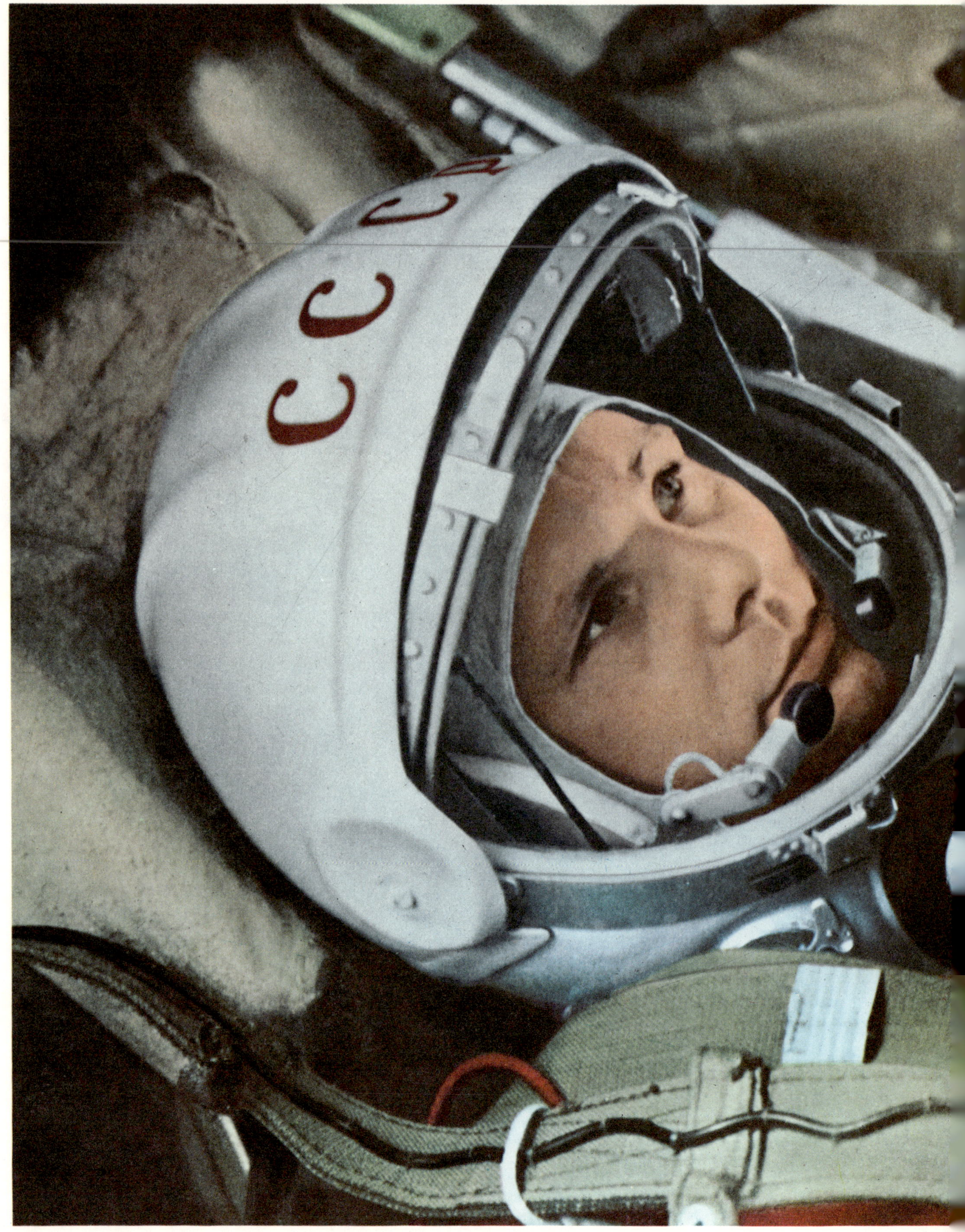
СССР

vised to postpone the flight, but he refused. On the morning of May 20, 1927, the *Spirit of St. Louis* took off from Roosevelt Field, New York, and headed toward the Atlantic Ocean.

For most of the first day nothing was heard of the pilot and his plane. Then a radio message was received announcing that Lindbergh had been spotted flying over St. John's, Newfoundland. From then on there was silence, while Lindbergh spent the first night in the middle of a hurricane, struggling against the need for sleep and against the icy winds that blew in through the windowless cockpit.

The world held its breath as radio announcers regularly interrupted their broadcasts to repeat the same words: "So far no news."

Then at last came the news that Lindbergh had landed at Le Bourget Field in Paris. It had taken him 33½ hours to make the journey. (It had taken Columbus almost 34 days.)

Perhaps the only time that Lindbergh feared for his safety was after he landed. Welcomed by 100,000 cheering Frenchmen, it took him half on hour to get from his plane to the ground as the admiring crowd passed him from hand to hand, sometimes turning him upside down.

## THE MOON IS NEAR

Lindbergh's flight, although a milestone, was soon surpassed by other aviators. For man was learning to move through the skies almost as easily as the birds he once envied. But another great adventure—a frightening and mysterious one—still beckoned. This was the conquest of space.

*Soviet cosmonaut Yuri A. Gagarin in the spacecraft Vostok I. In 1961 he became the first man to orbit the earth and return successfully.*

The pioneer in space travel was a Soviet Air Force officer, Yuri Gagarin. On April 12, 1961, he was launched into space aboard the Vostok I. Gagarin made one complete orbit (circle) of the earth at an average height of about 150 miles and a speed of about 17,000 miles an hour. This first spaceflight lasted 1 hour and 48 minutes.

Thus began a space race between the Soviet Union and the United States. On February 20, 1962, John Glenn, Jr., made the first orbit of the earth for the United States aboard the Mercury 6 space capsule. From then on record followed record. On March 18, 1965, Soviet cosmonaut Alexei Leonov left his capsule, Voskhod 2, which was piloted by Pavel

Belyayev, and, attached to a 16-foot line, "walked" in space for 10 minutes.

Not to be outdone, on June 3, 1965, American astronaut Edward White took a 20 minute "walk in space." The capsule was the Gemini 4, piloted by James McDivitt.

These experiments in space continued as man approached the goal of landing on the moon: there were successful dockings of vehicles in space; and the moon itself was orbited.

## THE MOON IS OURS!

On July 16, 1969, three American astronauts were launched from earth in the Apollo 11 spacecraft. Four days later, on July 20th, Neil Armstrong and Edwin ("Buzz") Aldrin set foot on the dusty surface of the moon and raised the Stars and Stripes. The moon was ours!

When I say "ours" I do not mean only the United States, but all the world.

Did the successful landing on the moon mean the end of our adventures in space? Hardly, it is only a start. We are beginning to probe the planets and even trying to establish some kind of communication with the distant stars.

But, you may ask: Is there no more room left on earth for adventure? Yes, there is. One last great adventure remains, and it is probably the most important of all. Perhaps it is the only one that is really worthwhile.

It is the discovery of man himself—of ourselves. And it is an adventure in which you will one day take part.

And I hope to be with you when you do. Your good friend Mickey Mouse sends you his love and all his best.

*Opposite page: The lunar rover. Carried aboard Apollo 15 in 1971, it was the first man-operated "car" to be used on the surface of the moon.*

# INDEX

**A**

Acropolis, Athens, 24
Africa, 9, 14, 15, 24, 41, 66, 67, 68, 77-80
Albuquerque, Affonso de, 68
  map of route, 66
Aldrin, Edwin, 123
Alexander the Great, 21, 22-27
  map of empire, 26-27
Alexandria, Egypt, 25
Ammon, oracle of, 26
Amon, Temple of, 12
Amundsen, Roald, 90, 93, 94, 95, 96, 97, 98, 99
Anderson, William R., 93
Andrée, Salomon August, 86
  balloon, 83
Antarctic Circle, 75
Antarctic exploration, 94-100
  map, 99
Apollo, Temple of, 21
Apollo 11, spacecraft, 123
Arabia, 27, 51
Arabs, 54, 68
Archeology, 30-37
Arctic exploration, 82-93
  map, 82
Arctic Ocean, 84
Aristotle, 22
Armstrong, Neil, 123
Artemis, Temple of, 20
Asia, 20, 24, 25, 46, 51, 56, 61
Asia Minor, 23, 24, 29
Athena, 24
Athens, Greece, 24
Atlantic Ocean, 56, 70, 108, 118, 121
Australia, 74, 75
Aviation, 117-121
Aztec Indians, 36

**B**

Babylon, Mesopotamia, 26, 27
Bahama Islands, 61, 62
Balloon, aircraft, 83, 86, 109, 116
Barbados, 111

Bathyscaphe, 109-110
Bathysphere, 108
Beardmore Glacier, 100
Beebe, William, 108
Belyayev, Pavel, 123
Bennett, James Gordon, 78
Bowers, Henry, 100
Britain, 29
British Isles, 16
Bucephalus, horse, 22, 24
Bulgaria, 23
Burma, 51
Byrd, Richard E., 93

**C**

Cabral, Pedro Alvarez de, 68
  map of route, 66
Cadiz, colony, 14
Caesar, Gaius Julius, 28-29
Calicut, India, 67
Cam, Diogo, 66
Camöens, Luis Vas de, 68
Canary Islands, 61
Cano, Juan Sebastian del, 73
*Capitana* see *Santa María*
Caravan, 9
Caravel, 60, 61, 63
Carthage, 14, 15-16
Caspian Sea, 26
Chacs, 36
Chaeronea, battle of, 22
Charles I, King of Spain, 70
Chichén Itzá, 36-37
China, 46, 51, 52, 62
Chomolungma see Everest, Mount
Cleopatra VII, Queen of Egypt, 29
Coal, 52
Columbus, Christopher, 44, 52, 54-64, 67, 111, 121
  maps, 57, 65
Compagnoni, Achille, 108
Cook, James, 74-75
Crassus, Marcus Licinius, 29
Crete, 34, 115, 116
Cuba, 62

**D**

Daedalus, 115, 116
Da Gama, Vasco see Gama
Dardanelles, Strait of the, 23, 24
Darius III, King of Persia, 24, 25, 26
Da Vinci, Leonardo, 116
Deep-sea exploration, 108-110
Denmark, 17, 43
Desio, Ardito, 108
Dias, Bartholomeu, 66, 67, 68
  map of route, 66
Dirigible, 90, 91, 93
*Discovery*, ship, 98

**E**

*Eagle*, balloon, 83, 86
Earth, 54, 74
Ecbatana, now Hamadan, Iran, 26
Egypt, 9, 11, 12, 14, 25, 29, 32, 111
Ellesmere Island, Canada, 89
Ellsworth, Lincoln, 90
El Tajín, pyramid, Mexico, 36
England, 74, 75, 78, 80, 96, 98
Ephesus, Asia Minor, 20
Eratosthenes, 54
Erebus, Mount, 99
Ericson, Leif, 44
Eric the Red, 44
Eskimo, 88, 89
Europe, 29, 41
Europeans, 54, 68
Evans, Arthur, 34
Evans, Edgar, 100
Everest, Mount, 105-06, 107
Explorers, 39-44, 54-101

**F**

Ferdinand II, King of Spain, 59, 62, 64
Flight, human, 115-121
Florence, Italy, 56
*Flyer*, aircraft, 117

*Fram*, ship, 84, 86, 94, 95
   bell, 87
Franz Josef Land, 86

## G

Gagarin, Yuri, *120-21*, 122
Gama, Vasco da, 67, 68
   map of route, *66*
Gaugamela, Mesopotamia, 26
Gaul, 29
Gedrosia desert, 27
Gemini 4, spacecraft, 123
Genoa, Italy, 52, *56*
Geography, 54, *56*
Glenn, John, Jr., 123
Glider, 117
Godwin Austen, Mount, 108
Gold, 16, 39, 62, 64
Good Hope, Cape of, 14, 66, 67, 68, 69
Gordian knot, 25
Gordium, Phrygia, 25
Granicus River, 25
Greece, 22-27, 29, 32, 34, 54
Greenland, 43, 44, 83, 84, 88
Guanahaní *see* Watling Island
Guinea, 15

## H

Haiti, 62, 64
Hanno, 15
   route of expedition, *16*
Hatshepsut, Queen of Egypt, 11, 12
Hawaiian Islands, 74, 75
Helicopter, 116
Hellespont *see* Dardanelles
Henson, Matthew, 89
Henu, 9, 11
Herodotus, 14, 15
Herostratus, 20
Heyerdahl, Thor, 110, 111
Hieroglyphics, 32
Hillary, Edmund, 106
Himalayas, 105, 106, *107*, 108
Hispaniola, now Haiti, 62
Hissarlik, Turkey, 34
H.M.S. *Endeavour*, ship, 75
Homer, 22, 32, 34
Horn, Cape, 75
Hunt, John, 106
Hydaspes, Kashmir, 27

## I

Icarus, 115, 116
Iceland, 44
*Iliad*, 22, 34
Illyrians, 22, 23
Inca Indians, 111

India, 27, 67, 68
Indian Ocean, 14, 67, 68
Indians of North America, 44, 62, 64
Indians of South America, 36, 111
Indies (Far East), 56, 64, 66, 68, 70
Indochina, 51
Indonesia, 46, 51
Isabella, Queen of Spain, 59, 62, 64
Issus, now Turkey, 25
*Italia*, dirigible, 93
Italy, 29, 46, 108

## J

Jackson, Frederick, 86
Jamaica, 64
Japan, 56, 62
Jaxartes (now Syr Darya) River, 26
Johansen, F.H., 84, 86
John II, King of Portugal, 59
Julian clan, 28

## K

K2 *see* Godwin Austen, Mount
Karakoram range, Himalayas, 108
Knossos, Crete, 34
*Kon-Tiki*, raft, *110*, 111
Kublai Khan, 46, 49, 51

## L

Labyrinth, 34, 115
Lacedelli, Lino, 108
*La Navidad*, colony, 64
Landa, Diego de, 36
Land of Punt (Somalia), 9, 11
Land of the Five Rivers *see* Punjab
Leif the Lucky *see* Ericson, Leif
Leonov, Alexei, 123
Lilienthal, Otto, 117
Lindbergh, Charles, 118, *119*, 121
Livingstone, David, 76, 77-80
Lunar rover, *122*
*Lusiadas, Os*, 68

## M

Macedonia, 22, 25, 27
Magellan, Ferdinand, 68, 70, 71, 72-73
   route of voyage, map, *70*
Malawi, Lake, Africa, 78

Malaya, 51
Manuel I, King of Portugal, 70
Marianas Islands, 72
Marianas Trench, 110
Marius, Gaius, 28
Massalia, now Marseilles, France, 16
Maya Indians, 36
McDivitt, James, 123
Mediterranean Sea, 13, 15, 25
Mercury 6, spacecraft, 123
Middle Ages, 54
Minos, King of Crete, 34, 115
Minotaur, 34
Moluccas, 68, 70, 73
Montgolfier, Joseph and Jacques-Etienne, 116
Moon landing, 123
Morocco, 111

## N

Nansen, Fridtjof, 83-84, *85*, 86, 94
Napoleon I, 32
*Nautilus see* U.S.S. *Nautilus*
Navigation, 43
Nepal, 105, 106
New Caledonia, 75
New Siberian Islands, 84
New South Wales, now Australia, 75
New World, 59, 61, 64, 111
New York City, 118, 121
New York *Herald*, 78
New Zealand, 74, 75, 98
Ngami, Lake, South Africa, 78
Nile River, 9, 12, 14, 78, 80
*Niña*, ship, *60*, 61, 64
Nobile, Umberto, 90, 93
Norfolk Island, 75
*Norge*, dirigible, 90, *91*, 93
Norkey, Tenzing, 106, *108*
Norsemen *see* Vikings
North Africa, 15, 111
North America, 43, 44, 75, 111
North Pole, 82, 84, 86, 88, 89, 90, 93, 94
Norway, 17, 43, 44, 83, 84, 86
Nuclear submarine, 92, 93
Nyasa, Lake, now Lake Malawi, 78

## O

Oates, Lawrence, 100
Obelisk, 12
Old World, 61
Olympias, Queen of Macedonia, 22
Oscar II, King of Norway, 84

125

## P

Pacific Ocean, 70, 72, 74, 75, 110, 111
   map, 72-73
Palermo, colony, 14
Palestine, 25, 51
Paper money, 52
Papyrus, 111
Paris, France, 118, 121
Peary, Robert Edward, 86, 88-90, 94
Pella, Macedonia, 22
Persepolis, Persia, 26
Persia, 24-27, 46, 51
Peru, 111
Pharnaces, 29
Philip II, King of Macedonia, 22
Philippines, 73
Phoenicians, 12-14, 25
   ship, 17
   shipbuilding, 12-13
Piccard, Auguste, 108, 109, 110
Piccard, Jacques, 109, 110
Pigafetta, Antonio, 70
*Pinta*, ship, 60, 61, 64
Pinzón, Martín Alonzo, 60
Pinzón, Vicente Yáñez, 60
Pirate, 41
Planets, 74, 75, 123
Plutarch, 22
Polo, Maffeo, 46, 51
Polo, Marco, 46-52, 56
   map of travels, 47
Polo, Niccolo, 46, 48, 51
Polynesia, 111
Pompey the Great, 29
Portugal, 56, 59, 66, 67, 68, 70
Porus, 27
Priam, King of Troy, 32
Puerto Rico, 64
Punjab, India, 24, 26-27
Punt (Somalia), 9, 11
Pytheas, 16, 17
   route of voyage, 16

## R

*Ra*, boat, 111
*Ra II*, boat, 111, *112*, *113*
Raven, 43
Red Sea, 11, 14
Rhine River, 29
Rome, 28, 29, 54
*Roosevelt*, ship, 89
Rosetta Stone, 32
Ross Sea, 95, 99

Rubicon, 29
Rumania, 23

## S

San Salvador, now Watling Island, 62
*Santa Clara see Niña*
*Santa María*, ship, 60, 61, 62
Santangel, Luis de, 59
Sataspes, 15
Schliemann, Heinrich, 32, 34
Scott, Robert Falcon, 96, 98, 99, 100, *101*
Scurvy, 67, 72, 75
Sheba, 9, 11
Sherpa, 106
South America, 64, 70, 72, 74
South Pole, 75, 90, 94-95, 96, 98, 99
   ice sheet, 96-97
South Seas, 75
Soviet Union, 123
Space travel, 122-23
Spain, 59, 64, 67, 70
Speke, John, 78
Spice Islands *see* Moluccas
Spices, 68, 70
*Spirit of St. Louis*, airplane, *118*, 121
Spitsbergen islands, 86
Stanley, Henry M., 78, 79, 80
Storms, Cape of *see* Good Hope, Cape of
Stratosphere, 109
Sudan, 9
Sun, 74
Susa, Persia, 26
Svalbard islands *see* Spitsbergen islands
Sverdrup, Otto, 84, 86
Sweden, 17

## T

Tahiti, 75
Tanganyika, Lake, 78
*Terra Nova*, ship, 98, 99
Thebes, Egypt, 12
Thebes, Greece, 22, 23
Thompson, Edward, 36, 37
Thrace, 22, 23
Thule, 17
Tibet, 105, 106
Tierra del Fuego, 72
Torres, Luis de, 62

Toscanelli, Paolo dal Pozzo, 56, 59
*Trieste*, bathyscaphe, *109*, 110
Trinidad, 64
Trireme, 24
Troy, Asia Minor, 24, 25, 32, 34
Tutankhamen, pharaoh of Egypt, 30
Tyre, 12-13, 25

## U

Ujiji, Tanzania, 78
Underwater exploration, 108-110
United States, 89, 123
U.S.S. *Nautilus*, 92, 93
Utica, North Africa, 14
Uxmal, Mexico, 32

## V

Valley of the Kings, Egypt, 33
Venice, Italy, 46, 51, 52
Venus, planet, 74
Vespucci, Amerigo, *65*, 70
*Victoria*, ship, 73
Victoria Falls, 78, *81*
Vikings, 41-44
   map, 41
Vinland, 44
Voskhod 2, spacecraft, 123
Vostok I, spacecraft, 122

## W

Walsh, Don, 110
Walvis Bay, South West Africa, 66
Watling Island, 62
West Africa, 15
White, Edward, 123
Wilson, Edward, 100
*Windward*, ship, 86
Wineland *see* Vinland
World, map, 52-53
Wright, Orville and Wilbur, *116*, 117, 118

## Y

Yucatan Peninsula, Mexico, 36
Yugoslavia, 23

## Z

Zambezi River, 78
Zeus, 26

126